DEMYSTIFYING THE STOCK MARKET

by John Charles Pool and Robert L. Frick

THE DURELL INSTITUTE OF MONETARY SCIENCE
at Shenandoah University

ISBN 1-882505-02-6

Printed in the United States of America

Produced by AAH Graphics (703) 933-6210

To Betty
and to Mike, Laura Linda and Jordan
and to Karen and Amy.
Our inspirations.

Acknowledgments

All books are the combined work of many more people than those whose names appear on the cover. That is true for this one more than most.

First, we want to thank Mrs. Elizabeth Racer, Director of the Durell Institute of Monetary Science, who originally conceived the idea and sponsored it. Also thanks to her friendly and always helpful staff including in particular Mrs. Kathleen Smith and Mrs. Dianne Singer. And, of course, the late George Edward Durell whose benevolence continues to support education in the fields of business, finance and economics. We all owe him a great debt.

A number of people generously helped with the details and logistics. They include: Theodore K. Levy, Vice President of Research for Sage, Rutty and Co., Inc. for keeping our focus on what really is important in the market; Ross M. LaRoe of Dennison University, who helped with the data analysis; Doyle Marker, an astute investor friend who reviewed the materials; Beth Guche of Eastside Secretarial Service who expertly prepared the manuscript for publication; Sheilah Reynolds of Brockport High School, Brockport, N.Y. who reviewed the materials from a teacher's perspective; and Allison Davies of Penfield High School, Penfield, N.Y. who gave us a student's reaction.

And special thanks to Jack Rosenberry of the *Democrat and Chronicle* and *Times-Union,* and Melissa L. Rosenberry. Their reviews and editing were invaluable.

Finally, we would like to acknowledge that this book may not make you rich; but at least if you're not, you'll know why.

For any errors or omissions, we dutifully acknowledge that they are ours.

Preface

Even though more people are investing in the financial markets than ever before, knowing the ins and outs of the financial markets is still thought of by many as a skill reserved for the rich and well-educated. But how did the rich get rich? And how did the well-educated pay for their degrees? Often through smart investing.

And smart investing is simply a little know-how, a little common sense and some patience. No knowledge of higher mathematics—and no luck—are required. Certainly some barriers exist to starting a good portfolio of investments that will beat inflation and taxes, and will become a deep well of money where college educations, house down payments and financial security can be drawn.

One of those barriers is the bewildering selection of investments from which to choose. Another is not knowing why securities behave as they do. In this book we hope to help readers cross those barriers by explaining how the markets work, what the advantages and disadvantages are of different investments, and how the economy and basic economic principles affect investments and financial markets.

But the highest barrier is simply the fear of making mistakes. Some trust an investment advisor such as a broker or financial planner with investment decisions in the hopes of eliminating that fear. But then the fear becomes whether the investment advisor is making the right decisions. Either way, some knowledge about markets, investments and economics is key to confident and fear-free investing.

This book, we hope, is another contribution to what is a rather large literature on the topic. We like to think it is different in the sense that it doesn't presume any prior knowledge on the topic. Instead it assumes that everyone has an interest in making money. That's what capitalism is all about.

Contents

Company Summary; Paychex, Inc.: Income Compared to Stock Prices, 1983–92; Paychex, Inc.: Balance Sheet for 1992.

Tables: Income Statement, Sweatshirt, Inc.; Balance Sheet, Sweatshirt, Inc.; Paychex, Inc.: Price/Income 1984–92.

3

THE FINANCIAL MARKETS

Introduction; History of the Markets; The New York Stock Exchange; The American Stock Exchange; The Crashes of 1929 and 1987; Regional Exchanges; How Stocks are Traded; The Over-the-Counter Market; The NASDAQ; Foreign Stock Markets; Penny Stocks; Bond Markets; Bond Prices and Ratings; U.S. Treasury Bonds; Futures Markets; Looking Ahead.

Figures: Location of Wall Street; Volume of Stocks Traded NYSE, OTC, AMEX, and Overseas; How to Read a Bond Table; How to Follow Treasury Bonds; How to Read Spot Market Prices in Newspaper; How to Read Commodity Future Prices; How to Read Stock Index Futures.

4

INVESTING THE EASY WAY

Introduction; What are Mutual Funds?; Why Buy Mutual Funds?; Different Types of Mutual Funds; Equity Funds; Bond Funds; Mixed Funds; Money Market Funds; Precious Metal Funds; Open-end and Closed-end Funds; How to Evaluate Mutual Funds; Performance; Stability; Costs; Which Funds are Best For You?; Risk-Free Investing; Building Your Portfolio; Investment Timing; Investing For the Long Term; Looking Ahead.

Figures: Sample Mutual Fund Table; ABC and XYZ Stock Prices; Average Rate of ABC and XYZ Stock Prices; Financial Industrial Income and 20th Century Ultra; Growth of Mutual Funds by Dollar Amount; Growth of Mutual Funds by Household Penetration; Percent of Money Held in Funds of Different Types; Forbes Mutual Fund Rating Sample; Sample Mutual Fund Prospectus Cover; The Effect of Taxes on an Investment Portfolio; Showing the Risk Versus Return Graph; The Risk Pyramid; Investment Mixes; Gains in Investments Over Long Periods.

Tables: Performance of Different Types of Funds Over Time.

5

6

7

Chapter 1

Let's Buy Some Stocks

In this chapter, we take a brief overview of investing in the stock market. We learn what stocks are, and why anyone would want to buy them. Then we look at how one goes about opening a brokerage account and buying some stocks. After that we imagine we have $15,000 to invest and use it to buy some stocks and mutual funds. Then, we learn a simple way to follow our stocks from the financial pages of our local newspapers by reading the stock tables. Finally, we learn how to calculate our gains —or losses.

INTRODUCTION

Nearly everyone knows that somewhere, in some mysterious place in New York City there is something called "the stock market," which is located on "Wall Street." And nearly everyone knows some people make a lot of money by investing in "the market."

Why is so much time and attention spent on stocks and stock markets? The answer is simple: Over time stocks can increase our wealth at a faster rate than other investments, such as bank accounts, U.S. Treasury securities and bonds. For example, if we had bought $1,000 worth of Walt Disney Company stock in 1982, by the end of 1992 those shares would have been worth $9,860.

If stocks can increase wealth so much faster than banks, why does anyone put their money in savings accounts? The answer is risk. Stocks can yield much more than safe investments such as banks and U.S. Treasury securities, but those alternatives are practically guaranteed (by the U.S. government) against losing the money you started with. Stocks have no such guarantees.

For example, if investors had put $1,000 in Eastern Airlines stock,

1

rather than Disney, in 1982, ten years later they would have had nothing, because Eastern went bankrupt in the late 1980s, making its stock worthless.

But for taking the risk of owning stocks and through wise investing, investors expect returns that exceed returns of safe investments. Stocks can produce these superior rewards because they tap into potent wealth-creating machines: corporations. By owning a share of a corporation's stock, you are not lending the corporation money, you literally own a piece of that business. You have a right to a small piece of the corporation's profits, and you own part of its buildings, of its land, even of its furniture.

But how do you get in on the action? How do you make money in the stock market? And, just as important: How do you keep from *losing* money in the stock market? In other words: How do you break into the mysterious world of investing in the financial markets?

As we shall soon see, it's not as difficult, or as mysterious as it seems. All you need is some money and some desire to get it working for you.

To be sure, the financial world is a complex place, full of esoteric words and strange practices such as options, warrants, puts and calls, program trading, mutual funds, arbitrage, and dollar averaging, to name but a few. Yet once you learn a little of the language, investing in the stock market is a simple, straightforward proposition. So before we look at the details, let's just jump right in and let's buy some stocks.

A SIMPLE STOCK MARKET GAME

The first thing we need, of course, is money. Let's assume you've saved $15,000, and wish to invest it where it can make more money than by just leaving it in the bank. So you turn to the stock market. That brings up the general problem of how to do it, and the specific problem of where to do it, which means you have to find a **stockbroker**; someone who has the connections and know-how to get your money invested in some stocks.

One alternative is to invest in stock mutual funds. Such a mutual fund contains many stocks, which are bought and sold by investment experts. Instead of buying individual stocks, you can buy shares in a mutual fund. And many funds offer direct investment, bypassing brokers. But, because a stockbroker can also help you select mutual funds, we'll start our investment journey by finding a stockbroker.

KEY CONCEPT: A STOCKBROKER IS SOMEONE WHO IS LICENSED AND REGISTERED TO BUY AND SELL STOCKS ON YOUR BEHALF.

Finding one of the many thousands of registered brokers in the United States is as easy as asking a friend to recommend one. Or you could ask a family accountant or lawyer to give you some names to check into. You may want to check the fees brokers charge (called commissions) before deciding which broker to choose. Commissions vary among brokers, and all things being equal, you want to pick a broker with lower commissions. Then simply call the office of the broker and set up an appointment.

Interestingly, this is one of those psychological barriers that a lot of people have—but they shouldn't. Many people think stockbrokers only deal with high-powered investors who have large amounts of money. But that's not the case at all. Some brokerage houses do have minimum deposit requirements to open an account, but many will accept an investment as low as $500, or less. Also, it's important to know that brokers earn a living from commissions they charge when they buy or sell stocks or other investments. So almost any broker will be happy to talk to you no matter how much money you have to invest. Furthermore, remember that while you may be starting out with a small amount of money, stockbrokers know that—chances are—later on many small investors become large investors. In addition, like any salesperson, a broker's objective is to build up his or her client list. The more clients they have, the more money they manage, and the more money they make. So, *don't be intimidated by the myth that stockbrokers only deal with large investors*. Take your checkbook and go out and find a broker. You'll get a friendly reception. We guarantee it.

DEALING WITH A STOCKBROKER

Now let's assume you have found a broker and have made an appointment to discuss your investment options. What should you expect next?

First of all, in order to give you sound advice, a broker is going to want to know a little bit about your financial situation. Most brokers may suggest that you have some money set aside in a bank account to cover your expenses for a few months (three to six months usually) in case you lose your income unexpectedly. Some may suggest that you think about investing a set amount, say, $100 a month, regularly in your brokerage account to help it grow over the years. This kind of advice varies with brokers and, in any case, it is *optional* for you. If you don't want advice, don't ask for it, and any broker will be happy to arrange to invest your money however you want.

Whatever the case, however, you will be asked to fill out an applica-

Account Application

For Office
Use Only:

In order for your account to be opened promptly and accurately, please provide _____ with all the information requested below. See back page for detailed instructions.

Type of Account You Are Opening

Registration: ☐ Individual   ☐ Tenants In Common*   ☐ Corporation or Partnership*
               ☐ Joint Tenants with Rights of Survivorship   ☐ Custodian for Minor   ☐ Trust*

Type: ☐ Cash   ☐ Margin   ☐ Option Trading*

*Additional documents are required to open these accounts. To request these forms, please call

Account Owner Information

		Social Security or
Account Owner's Name	Date of Birth	Taxpayer Identification Number

		Social Security or
Joint Account Owner's Name	Date of Birth	Taxpayer Identification Number

Mailing Address	City	State	ZIP Code

Home Address (if different from Mailing Address)	City	State	ZIP Code

Daytime   Evening
Phone (   )   Phone (   )   Citizenship: ☐ U.S.   ☐ Resident Alien   ☐ Non-Resident Alien

Your Employment Information

If you are not employed (such as retired, a student or a homemaker), please see instructions on back page.

Account Owner's Employer

Employer's Complete Address
City, State, ZIP Code   Telephone Number (   )

Occupation   Years Employed

Joint Account Owner's Employer

Employer's Complete Address
City, State, ZIP Code   Telephone Number (   )

Occupation   Years Employed

If you or a member of your immediate family is affiliated with or employed by a   Company _____
member of a stock exchange, bank, trust company, insurance company or the
National Association of Securities Dealers, please specify the company and   Position _____
your relationship to that family member and their position.   Relationship

If you are a director, 10% shareholder or officer of a publicly traded company,   Company _____
please specify the company.   Position _____

Financial Information (This Is Required Information)

Account Owner's Annual Income			Account Owner's Net Worth		
☐ $0 - $20,000	☐ $20,000 - $30,000	☐ $30,000 - $50,000	☐ $0 - $20,000	☐ $20,000 - $30,000	☐ $30,000 - $100,000
☐ $50,000 - $100,000	☐ $100,000 - $250,000	☐ Over $250,000	☐ $100,000 - $250,000	☐ $250,000 - $1 million	☐ Over $1 million

Figure 1-1, Sample brokerage account application.

tion. (See Figure 1-1: Sample Brokerage Account Application.) It will ask
you for some basic financial information and, perhaps, for some credit ref-
erences, usually something about your investment goals and strategies, and

how much you plan to invest initially. That's all there is. Just a simple application, which can be filled out in a few minutes.

DECIDING WHAT TO BUY

Now comes decision time. We've already established that you want to invest $15,000. The problem is: What to invest it in? Here your broker will explain that there are many different options, depending on your goals and the level of risk that you want to assume. The options include investing directly in the stock of only one company, or several; indirectly in a stock mutual fund that may invest in hundreds of companies; in bonds; or in a number of other alternatives we'll explain in later chapters. But to keep this simple, let's assume for now that you have already decided you want to invest part of your money in a **mutual fund** and the rest in **common stocks.**

KEY CONCEPT: A MUTUAL FUND IS A FINANCIAL COMPANY
THAT SELLS SHARES AND USES THE FUNDS PEOPLE PAY FOR
THOSE SHARES TO INVEST IN A WIDE RANGE OF COMMON
STOCKS OR OTHER KINDS OF SECURITIES.

KEY CONCEPT: A COMMON STOCK IS A SHARE OF OWNERSHIP
IN A CORPORATION, WHICH MAY PAY A DIVIDEND ANNUALLY.
ITS PRICE VARIES ACCORDING TO MANY FACTORS, INCLUDING
HOW PROFITABLE THE COMPANY IS, THE GENERAL STATE OF
THE COMPANY, THE DIVIDENDS IT PAYS AND THE LAWS OF
SUPPLY AND DEMAND.

Most brokers will suggest that a beginning investor buy stocks in mutual funds and/or in well-established companies in several different industries, so as to *diversify* your portfolio. By spreading your investment among different companies, proper **diversification** minimizes the risk of loss. Now you have the option of choosing among hundreds of companies, and many different industries. See, for example, the list of different industries shown in Table 1-1. But, in order to make a simpler exercise out of this, we're going to give you a list to choose from, recognizing that in the real world your options are much broader. You can pick any of the 50 stocks shown in Table 1-2, or you can follow along with us as we choose a diversified investment portfolio consisting of part stock mutual fund and stocks in three fictitious corporations.

Table 1-1

INDUSTRIES IN ALPHABETICAL ORDER

Advertising
Aerospace/Defense
Air Transport
Aluminum
Apparel
Auto & Truck
Auto & Truck (Foreign)
Auto Parts
Bank
Beverage (Alcoholic)
Beverage (Soft Drink)
Broadcasting/Cable TV
Building Materials
Canadian Energy
Cement & Aggregates
Chemical
Coal/Alternate Energy
Computers & Peripherals
Computer Software
Copper
Drug
Drugstore
Electric Equipment
Electric Utility
Electronics
Environmental
Financial Services
Food Processing
Food Wholesalers
Furn./Home Furnishings
Gold/Silver Mining
Grocery
Home Appliance
Homebuilding
Hotel/Gaming
Household Products

Housing
Industrial Services
Insurance
Investment Companies
Machinery
Machine Tool
Maritime
Medical Services
Medical Supplies
Metal Fabricating
Metals & Mining
Newspaper
Office Equip. & Supplies
Oilfield Services/Equip.
Packaging & Container
Paper & Forest Products
Petroleum
Precision Instrument
Recreation
Restaurant
Retail Building Supply
Retail (Special Lines)
Retail Store
Securities Brokerage
Semiconductor
Shoe
Steel
Telecom. Equipment
Telecom. Services
Textile
Thrift
Tire & Rubber
Tobacco
Toiletries/Cosmetics
Toys & School Supplies
Trucking/Transp. Leasing

KEY CONCEPT: DIVERSIFICATION MEANS SPREADING YOUR RISK
AMONG DIFFERENT INVESTMENTS.

You've got $15,000 to invest, so we'll start by guaranteeing a well-diversified portfolio by investing about a third of your money in a mutual fund. Mutual funds are run by investment experts, who shoulder the job of picking which stocks to buy and when to sell them. But because we want to manage some of our own stocks, with what remains we'll pick three corporations in different industries and invest about a third of what's left of your money in each. How many shares you will own will, of course, depend

Table 1-2

SELECTED STOCKS

1	AXP	American Express Co.	26	KR	The Kroger Co.
2	T	AT&T	27	MHS	Marriott Corp.
3	AVP	Avon Products, Inc.	28	MAT	Mattel, Inc.
4	BDK	Black & Decker Corp.	29	MYG	Maytag Corp.
5	BA	Boeing Company	30	MCD	McDonald's Corp.
6	CCI	Citicorp	31	MER	Merrill Lynch Co.
7	KO	Coca-Cola Co.	32	MOT	Motorola, Inc.
8	CL	Colgate-Palmolive Co.	33	NKE	Nike, Inc.
9	DAL	Delta Airlines, Inc.	34	OCF	Owens-Corning
10	DIS	Walt Disney Co.	35	PPG	PPG Industries
11	DOW	Dow Chemical Co.	36	PEP	PepsiCo, Inc.
12	DD	E.I. Dupont	37	PEF	Pfizer, Inc.
13	EK	Eastman Kodak	38	PG	Proctor & Gamble
14	FPP	Fisher Price	39	ROK	Rockwell Intl.
15	F	Ford Motor Co.	40	SLE	Sara Lee Corp.
16	GE	General Electric Co.	41	SPP	Scott Paper Co.
17	GIS	General Mills, Inc.	42	S	Sears Roebuck & Co.
18	GM	General Motors Corp.	43	TAN	Tandy Corp.
19	G	The Gillette Co.	44	TX	Texaco
20	HSY	Hershey Foods Corp	45	TOY	Toys "R" Us
21	HNZ	J.J. Heinz Co.	46	UIS	Unisys
22	IBM	Intl. Business Machines	47	U	US Air Group, Inc.
23	IP	International Paper Co.	48	X	USX Corp.
24	JNJ	Johnson & Johnson	49	WIN	WinDixie Suprmrkts.
25	KM	K-Mart Corp.	50	XRX	Xerox Corp.

on the price of each company's stock on the day you buy it. Then we'll follow your stocks for a period of one year, using their performance in 1992 as an example.

We choose three different industries because of that key word, *diversification*. If all our stocks were in one industry, say, the automobile industry, and car sales slumped, all of our stocks' prices might drop at the same time.

CHOOSING STOCKS

First, we have to decide in which industries we want to invest. That choice will depend on our perception of how those industries are doing and how they might do in the future. If, for example, an industry in general is not doing well for whatever reason we want to avoid it. On the other hand, if you think an industry has a bright future such as, say, the computer industry seems to have, you may want to be in on it. But you still have to be selective.

For now, to avoid the problem of selection strategies (which are discussed in Chapter 5), let's pick three fictitious corporations in three different industries. We'll take **Aardvark, Inc.** from the construction industry. Then **Burp—less, Inc.**, one of the largest corporations in the pharmaceuticals industry.

And finally, we'll choose **Caramba, Inc.** from the food industry. All are listed on the New York Stock Exchange under the symbols AAR, BURP and CAR respectively.

Aardvark, Inc.

52 Weeks					Yld		Vol				Net
Hi	Lo	Stock	Sym	Div	%	PE	100s	Hi	Lo	Close	Change
29⅞	14⅜	Aard	AAR	.40	1.2	22	18957	29⅝	28	28⅝	−1

Burp—less, Inc.

52 Weeks					Yld		Vol				Net
Hi	Lo	Stock	Sym	Div	%	PE	100s	Hi	Lo	Close	Change
35⅞	24¼	Burp	BURP	401	1.3	23	9558	30¼	28¾	28⅛	+⅜

Caramba, Inc.

52 Weeks					Yld		Vol				Net
Hi	Lo	Stock	Sym	Div	%	PE	100s	Hi	Lo	Close	Change
90¼	12⅜	Cara	CAR	.80	1.1	16	1849	40½	40	40⅛	−¾

On January 2nd, 1992 Aardvark common stocks were selling for $28.63; Burp—less was priced at $28.13, and Caramba at $40.13. With the

Table 1-3

PORTFOLIO SUMMARY:
JANUARY 2, 1992

INVESTMENTS OWNED

Initial Deposit	$15,000.00
Commissions	–270.00
Total Account Value	$14,730.00
Net Portfolio Value	$14,688.00
Ending Cash Balance	$ 42.00

PORTFOLIO POSITION DETAIL

CATEGORY	SYMBOL	QUANTITY	DES	PRICE	MARKET VALUE
Stocks	AAR	100	Aardvark	$28.63	$ 2862.50
	BURP	100	Burp—less	$28.13	$ 2812.50
	CAR	100	Caramba	$40.13	$ 4013.00
Net Stock Portfolio Value					$ 9688.00
W-M Mutual Fund, 2500 shares at $20.00					$ 5000.00
					$14,688.00

$10,000 we have to invest in stocks we can buy 100 shares of Aardvark, 100 shares of Burp—less and 100 shares of Caramba. What is left we'll invest in a mutual fund, say the W-M Mutual Fund—the W-M meaning "well-managed."

Now we give our broker a check for $15,000 and he buys the stocks and mutual fund shares for us using a computerized system that purchases the stocks almost immediately. If we wish we can have the stock certificates sent directly to us and put them in a safety deposit box or somewhere else for safekeeping. But, more likely, we will let our brokerage house hold them for us to avoid all that hassle, and the possibility of losing them.

Now our business with the broker is done. In a few days we will receive a statement from the brokerage house showing what was bought and at exactly what price. It will look something like Table 1-3. After that we'll get a similar statement each month, showing the status of our account and how much the stock price and the value of our portfolio increased (or decreased) over the previous month. If we are going to be passive investors concerned only with long-term gains, that will be enough to keep us informed about how our investment portfolio is gaining (or losing).

Keeping Track of Your Investments

Most investors like to follow their investments closely, so we need to know how to keep track of the stocks we own on a daily basis. After all, if one is not doing so well, we might decide to sell it and buy something else. Now that our brokerage account is set up we could do that with a simple phone call to our broker, who would be happy to make the trade. He also might give us some advice as to whether he thought that was a prudent move. But, remember, every time we trade commissions are involved and they can eat into our profits.

We bought 100 shares of Aardvark, 100 of Burp—less and 100 of Caramba at prices of $28.63, 28.13, and $40.13 respectively, at the beginning of 1992. Now we want to know how they're doing. To find out all we have to do is look at the stock tables in our local newspaper, or in one of the financial newspapers such as *The Wall Street Journal*. All of our stocks are listed on the New York Stock Exchange (NYSE), so that makes it easy. The problem of deciphering the tables is a bit more complicated, but not really very difficult.

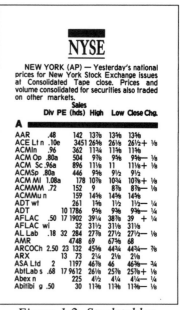

Figure 1-2, Stock tables.

DECIPHERING THE STOCK TABLES

The stock tables look a bit formidable at first glance (see Figure 1-2 for example), but they really aren't all that complicated. In fact, they give a lot of information in a very small space. Let's see what all those numbers and symbols mean.

52 Weeks					Yld		Vol			Net	
Hi	Lo	Stock	Sym	Div	%	PE	100s	Hi	Lo	Close	Change

First let's take a look at a typical stock listing and see what it tells us. We'll use the large media company, Gannett, which publishes more than 90 newspapers, including USA TODAY, as an example.

52 Weeks				Yld		Vol			Net	
Hi	Lo	Stock Sym	Div	%	PE	100s	Hi	Lo	Close	Change
55	41	Gannett GCI	1.28	2.5	21	3311	50	49	50	+1

What do the stock tables tell us about Gannett? A lot. First of all we can see that for the preceding 52 weeks Gannett common stock price varied from as **high** as $55 to as **low** as $41. Then we can see that Gannett's **estimated dividend** for this year is $1.28 per share. That's a check mailed to you, if you own the stock. Next is the dividend expressed as a percentage rate of return, or a **yield** of 2.5 percent in this case. This is simply the dividend divided by the closing price.

Then we have the **price/earnings ratio,** which is the ratio of the price of one share of stock to the company's annual earnings per share. In this case Gannett stock is selling for about 21 times its earnings. The price/earnings ratio is a useful bit of information because it gives us a sense of what the market thinks the value of the stock is compared to the value of other stocks. Next there's some simpler stuff.

The **volume** (3311) tells you how many shares were traded the previous day. To get this figure add two zeros. On that day some 331,100 shares of Gannett stock were traded. The volume of shares traded gives us some sense of how much interest there is in the stock. An increase in volume tells us that something—either bad or good—possibly is going on with that company. Then the next two columns tell us the **high** (50) and the **low** (49) price that the stock traded for that day. Then, there is the **closing price**, the price at which the stock closed that day. Finally, we have the **Net Change,** the amount that the price went up or down at its closing from the previous day's closing price. That, of course, tells us how much we gained or lost that day if we owned the stock.

One little side point needs to be made here. You've probably noticed that stock prices are quoted in fractions. The reason is that before the age of computers it was easier to calculate them that way, and although it's no longer necessary the exchanges continue to use this system as a matter of tradition. So, clumsy as it seems, that's something you have to get used to if you're going to play the stock market. To convert the fractions to cents you divide the denominator into the numerator. This is done in Table 1-4.

KEEPING TRACK OF YOUR INVESTMENTS

To say the least, it's interesting how much information you can learn about a company from that little line in the stock tables! Now let's put our new knowledge to work and take a closer look at the three stocks we bought.

First, let's find Aardvark and see what the tables tell us. When we first bought the stock at the beginning of 1992 AAR looked like this:

Aardvark, Inc.

52 Weeks					Yld		Vol				Net
Hi	Lo	Stock	Sym	Div	%	PE	100s	Hi	Lo	Close	Change
27⅞	14⅜	AARD	AAR	.40	1.2	22	18957	29⅝	28	28⅝	−1

Mostly we're interested in the price and the change from the previous day. That's easy enough to find. The current price is $28.63 at the *close* of the market on January 2nd, 1992. The gain (or loss in this case) was -1, from the day before.

Now we have established a base line, the Aardvark price at the beginning of the year. Then we need to do the same thing for our other two stocks. Burp—less sold for 28⅛ when we bought it, and Caramba for 40⅛.

Given that we know where we started, the problem is to find a simple way to see where we're going. What we're interested in is how the prices of our stocks are changing and how that affects the value of our portfolio.

For this, we can set up a worksheet such as the ones shown in Tables 1-5, 6 and 7.

All we have to do is record the price of the stock the day we bought it and multiply by the number of shares we bought to get the total value of our investment in that stock. Then we need to calculate the percentage change from our original investment to any future date we want.

Calculating the percentage change is important because change is what counts, not actual dollar values. If a stock is priced at $100 then an increase of $5 is a 5 percent change, which is significant, but not a major event. But if a stock is priced at $10 and its price increases by $5, that's a 50 percent increase and that *is* a major

Table 1-4:

FRACTIONS TO DECIMALS

$1/16$ = .0625
$1/8$ = .1250
$3/16$ = .1875
$1/4$ = .2500
$5/16$ = .3125
$3/8$ = .3750
$7/16$ = .4375
$1/2$ = .5000
$9/16$ = .5625
$5/8$ = .6250
$11/16$ = .6875
$3/4$ = .7500
$13/16$ = .8125
$7/8$ = .8750
$15/16$ = .9375

event, a signal that something important is happening with that stock.

KEY CONCEPT: PERCENTAGE CHANGE IS CALCULATED BY
SUBTRACTING THE ORIGINAL PRICE FROM THE CURRENT PRICE
AND DIVIDING THE CHANGE BY THE ORIGINAL PRICE.

$$\text{PERCENTAGE CHANGE} = \frac{\textit{CURRENT PRICE} - \textit{ORIGINAL PRICE}}{\textit{ORIGINAL PRICE}}$$

In Tables 1-5, 6 and 7 we have worked out some examples of what

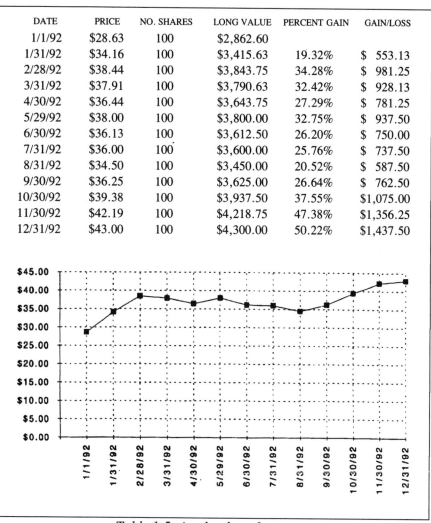

DATE	PRICE	NO. SHARES	LONG VALUE	PERCENT GAIN	GAIN/LOSS
1/1/92	$28.63	100	$2,862.60		
1/31/92	$34.16	100	$3,415.63	19.32%	$ 553.13
2/28/92	$38.44	100	$3,843.75	34.28%	$ 981.25
3/31/92	$37.91	100	$3,790.63	32.42%	$ 928.13
4/30/92	$36.44	100	$3,643.75	27.29%	$ 781.25
5/29/92	$38.00	100	$3,800.00	32.75%	$ 937.50
6/30/92	$36.13	100	$3,612.50	26.20%	$ 750.00
7/31/92	$36.00	100	$3,600.00	25.76%	$ 737.50
8/31/92	$34.50	100	$3,450.00	20.52%	$ 587.50
9/30/92	$36.25	100	$3,625.00	26.64%	$ 762.50
10/30/92	$39.38	100	$3,937.50	37.55%	$1,075.00
11/30/92	$42.19	100	$4,218.75	47.38%	$1,356.25
12/31/92	$43.00	100	$4,300.00	50.22%	$1,437.50

Table 1-5, Aardvark performance.

happened with the three stocks we owned during 1992. At the end of this book there are some blank "stock tracking" forms that you can use to track the stocks you buy, either for real or hypothetically, if you have decided to try a simulation before you actually invest any real money, which we highly recommend.

Also, if you want to get a bit more sophisticated you might try making a chart out of your data, as we have done below the tables. This shows you

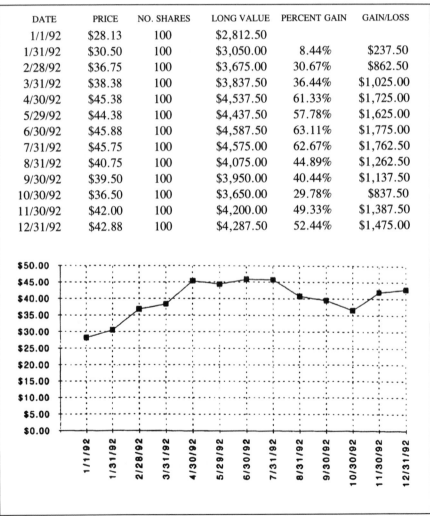

DATE	PRICE	NO. SHARES	LONG VALUE	PERCENT GAIN	GAIN/LOSS
1/1/92	$28.13	100	$2,812.50		
1/31/92	$30.50	100	$3,050.00	8.44%	$237.50
2/28/92	$36.75	100	$3,675.00	30.67%	$862.50
3/31/92	$38.38	100	$3,837.50	36.44%	$1,025.00
4/30/92	$45.38	100	$4,537.50	61.33%	$1,725.00
5/29/92	$44.38	100	$4,437.50	57.78%	$1,625.00
6/30/92	$45.88	100	$4,587.50	63.11%	$1,775.00
7/31/92	$45.75	100	$4,575.00	62.67%	$1,762.50
8/31/92	$40.75	100	$4,075.00	44.89%	$1,262.50
9/30/92	$39.50	100	$3,950.00	40.44%	$1,137.50
10/30/92	$36.50	100	$3,650.00	29.78%	$837.50
11/30/92	$42.00	100	$4,200.00	49.33%	$1,387.50
12/31/92	$42.88	100	$4,287.50	52.44%	$1,475.00

Table 1-6, Burp—less performance.

more graphically how your investment is doing. If your trend line is up, you're doing OK. If it's down, you might want to re-think your investment strategy.

Now let's look a little more carefully at what happened to our investment portfolio over the year. Our Aardvark stock increased by 50 percent for a gain of $1,437.50. Burp—less increased by 52 percent for a gain of $1,475.00. But Caramba, Inc. *decreased* by 32.27 percent. The combination

DATE	PRICE	NO. SHARES	LONG VALUE	PERCENT GAIN	GAIN/LOSS
1/1/92	$40.13	100	$4,013.00		
1/31/92	$40.73	100	$4,073.00	1.50%	$60.00
2/28/92	$39.28	100	$3,928.00	–2.12%	($85.00)
3/31/92	$35.43	100	$3,543.00	–11.71%	($470.00)
4/30/92	$32.33	100	$3,233.00	–19.44%	($780.00)
5/29/92	$31.30	100	$3,130.00	–22.00%	($883.00)
6/30/92	$29.13	100	$2,913.00	–27.41%	($1,100.00)
7/31/92	$33.14	100	$3,314.00	–17.42%	($699.00)
8/31/92	$36.57	100	$3,657.00	–8.87%	($356.00)
9/30/92	$28.75	100	$2,875.00	–28.36%	($1,138.00)
10/30/92	$28.15	100	$2,815.00	–29.85%	$1,198.00)
11/30/92	$28.01	100	$2,801.00	–30.20%	($1,212.00)
12/31/92	$27.18	100	$2,718.00	–32.27%	($1,295.00)

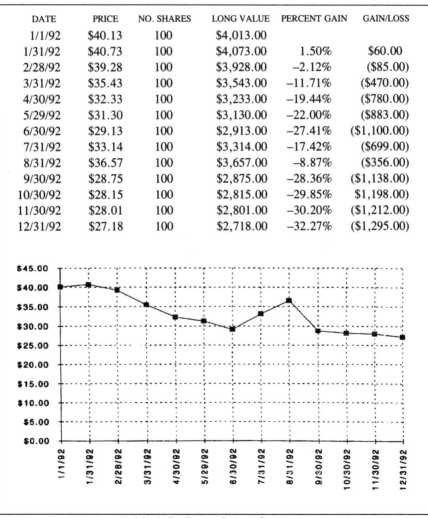

Table 1-7, Caramba performance.

Table 1-8

SELECTED MUTUAL FUND PERFORMANCE

NAME OF FUND	PERFORMANCE	1988	1989	1990	1991	1992
Fidelity Advisor Equity: Growth Inst.	199%	15.6%	44.8%	6.9%	64.7%	10.0%
Fidelity Contrafund	193%	20.9%	43.3%	3.9%	54.9%	15.9%
Pasadena Growth	171%	35.8%	37.7%	–4.6%	67.8%	2.2%
Brandywine	155%	17.7%	32.9%	0.6%	49.2%	15.6%
Meridian	152%	18.1%	19.5%	3.8%	58.0%	15.5%
IDEX II Growth	147%	20.5%	44.6%	–0.6%	58.7%	1.2%
Strong Discovery	143%	24.5%	24.0%	–2.8%	68.6%	2.0%
S&P 500	100%	17.5%	31.7%	3.12%	30.5%	7.6%

of two gainers and one loser left us with a net gain in our stock portfolio of $1617.50. Not a bad performance for a beginner. This shows, among other things, the importance of diversifying our portfolio. If we had invested all of our money in Caramba, we would have experienced a considerable loss. The rest of our money went into a growth-oriented mutual fund such as those shown in Table 1-8. Depending on which one we chose, our gain during 1992 would have ranged from a low of 1.2 percent to a high of 15.9 percent. Our selection: "W-M Mutual Fund" increased in value by 15 percent during 1992. Based on that performance our portfolio at the end of 1992 is shown in Table 1-9. Overall our gain based on our original investment of $15,000.00 was $2,098.76, or just under 21 percent for the year.

LOOKING AHEAD

So now we've learned how to invest in the stock market and how to keep track of our investment portfolio—all at the simplest level possible. Our next task is to find out a little more about what it is that we have been doing and how that fits into the overall scheme of things. Then we'll want to learn more about the stock exchanges and how they work, mutual funds, investing strategies, and the sophisticated tricks of the trade that professional investors use to make their investments even more profitable—sometimes. Finally, we'll look at how to follow the market, how the stock market relates to the overall health of the economy, and how we can forecast economic trends.

Table 1-9

PORTFOLIO SUMMARY:
DECEMBER 31, 1992

INVESTMENTS OWNED

Net Portfolio Value	$17,055.50
Ending Cash Balance (3% interest)	$ 43.26
TOTAL ACCOUNT VALUE	$17,098.76

PORTFOLIO POSITION DETAIL

CATEGORY	SYMBOL	QUANTITY	DES	PRICE	MARKET VALUE
Stocks	AAR	100	Aardvark	$43.00	$ 4,300.00
	BURP	100	Burp—less	$42.88	$ 4,287.00
	CAR	100	Caramba	$27.18	$ 2,718.00
Net Stock Portfolio Value					$11,305.50
W-M Mutual Fund, 250 shares at $23.00					$ 5,750.00
					$17,055.50

Chapter 2

Capitalism in Action

*In this chapter we take a brief look at the capitalist system, explore
how it works, and why. In particular we look at the role of
entrepreneurs, the capitalists who risk their time and money to
start new companies in the hope of making profits. Then we
examine the details of starting a new company, issuing stock and
selling it to the public. Finally, we look at some of the nitty-gritty
of the financial aspects of running a company with a focus on
understanding annual reports and financial statements.*

HOW CAPITALISM WORKS

Capitalism is an economic system in which everything needed to produce goods or services is owned by private individuals, as opposed to the only other alternative, being owned by the government.

KEY CONCEPT: CAPITALISM IS AN ECONOMIC SYSTEM IN WHICH
THE FACTORS OF PRODUCTION ARE OWNED BY PRIVATE
INDIVIDUALS.

If you stop and think about it, you will realize that in order to produce any product—any good or service—four things are required. One is **land**, by which is meant some space and/or some natural resources. Another is **labor**, some people willing to spend their time working on the production of the product. Another is **capital**, the plant and equipment (usually tools and machinery) needed. And, finally, we need the know-how to do it—the **technical knowledge** and skills necessary to combine the other factors together efficiently to produce the product. But more than mixing these resources goes on in our capitalist system. Money is involved, and so is risk.

19

KEY CONCEPT: THE FACTORS OF PRODUCTION ARE LAND,
LABOR, CAPITAL, AND THE TECHNICAL SKILL NEEDED TO
COMBINE THEM EFFICIENTLY TO ACHIEVE A DESIRED OUTPUT.

ENTREPRENEURSHIP

Money is required to buy and control the factors of production, and those who put up the money run the risk of losing it. Those who are willing to invest their money to start a business are called **entrepreneurs**[*]. They may be people who own businesses and employ others to manage it, or they may also help run the business. Either way they bear the risk of losing their investment if the business doesn't succeed. Of course, they share in the profits if it does well.

KEY CONCEPT: ENTREPRENEURS ARE THOSE WHO ARE WILLING
TO RISK THEIR TIME AND MONEY TO START A NEW BUSINESS.

You don't have to be an entrepreneur to participate in the capitalist system. Indeed, most of us are involved in capitalism in other ways. For example, we can buy land and rent it to entrepreneurs. Or, we can sell our labor and work for a wage or salary, which is the most common way most of us participate. Or, we can loan money to a company or individuals and receive interest payments. Or, we can buy stock and become a part owner of a company, in which case we share the profits—and the losses—with the entrepreneur who started it. The latter is our primary concern here.

WHAT IT MEANS TO BUY STOCKS

In the previous chapter when we bought imaginary stocks in Aardvark, Burp-less and Caramba, we became a part owner of those corporations. That meant we owned a small (probably very small) part of anything those companies own, be it a building, some machinery, or a car or truck. It also meant we had a right to share in any dividends those companies aid out of their profits, and a right to voice our opinions about how the company is managed.

ISSUING NEW STOCK

Why would a company want to sell part of itself to outside investors?

---

* After the French word meaning "to undertake."

Why would it let you have a say in how the company is run? Because, at some point it needed to raise money, either to get the company started, or to expand its operations in an attempt to increase its profits.

Before we examine that process we need to clarify that the word capital has two meanings. Capital refers to the plant and equipment (such as buildings and machinery) needed in the production process. But, the word capital also describes the money required to buy and control the factors of production. So there is a distinct and important difference between these two definitions. Real, or physical capital is one thing; financial capital is another.

KEY CONCEPT: REAL CAPITAL IS PLANT AND EQUIPMENT.
FINANCIAL CAPITAL IS THE MONEY NEEDED TO CONTROL THE
FACTORS OF PRODUCTION.

Usually companies issue stock to raise money. To see how this works, let's imagine you have just invented and patented a new mousetrap, one that will trap a mouse, vaporize it and transport its remains to Mars. You know these will be a big seller if you can just make them in large quantities. You want to start a new company, which you are going to call "Mickey Mousetrap, Inc." But you need money; that is, you need some capital funds in order to buy some capital goods.

One way to get it would be to go to a bank and borrow some money. But a bank might have some doubts about how well your new mousetrap is going to work. And they are going to want to know a lot about your personal financial situation. And, most likely, they will want some collateral to secure your investment. That means you may have to put up your house, or any other assets you may have, as security for a bank loan. You don't want to do that so, instead, you decide to start your own company and sell shares in it to outside investors.

To do that you have to file papers with the state you reside in to incorporate your company, and you will have to pay a small fee. Now you are ready to sell shares in an initial public offering (IPO). Let's say you need to raise $1,000,000 to launch this business. One way to approach this would be to find ten people each with $100,000 to invest as **venture capitalists**. Each of them would then own 10 percent of your company. But then you wouldn't own any of it. So, most likely, you will keep some of the stock for yourself and sell the rest, or you might invest some of your own money. Either way, you want to retain some ownership yourself, or none of this would make any sense. Let's say you invest $500,000 of your own money, which gives you half ownership, and want to sell the rest to investors. Now you have a strategy problem.

KEY CONCEPT: VENTURE CAPITALISTS ARE INVESTORS WHO FOCUS ON INVESTING IN NEW, OFTEN RISKY, BUSINESS VENTURES.

If you issue 10 shares of stock at $100,000 and buy five shares yourself then you have to find five investors to put up $100,000 each, and they would each own 10 percent of the company. Finding five investors to put $100,000 each into a new mousetrap company would not be easy, so instead you would probably decide to issue more shares at a lower price, say 10,000 shares at $100 each and buy 5,000 yourself. Now your sales job is easier because a lot more people would be willing to buy smaller amounts of the stock at the lower price.

Let's say you create 10,000 shares at $100 each. Each share of stock then represents a small percentage ownership in the company. Once the stock is issued and sold you have raised the money you need to launch the company, but now you have some problems—bosses to contend with.

ESTABLISHING A BOARD OF DIRECTORS

With 5,000 shares held internally, that is, by you as an "insider", there are 5,000 shares sold to the public, or what is called "floating" in the market. The owners of the floating shares will most likely not be interested in managing the company directly. Instead, they will want to elect a board of directors to oversee its operations.

In a small company situation a Board of Directors is generally made up of stockholders who have a vote on the board proportional to the number of shares they own. They, too, will not want to participate directly in the day-to-day management of the company. Instead, most likely they will elect a Chairman of the Board to perform that function. And he or she will probably appoint a president as General Manager or Chief Executive Officer (CEO) of the company. Under normal circumstances, since you want to manage the company (and own 50 percent of it), you would be named president. In that role you would be expected to report to the Chairman of the Board on a regular basis, and to the entire board at monthly or quarterly meetings.

DIVIDENDS AND RETAINED EARNINGS

Once your company is up and running and (let's assume) profitable then you have to contend with the question of what to do with the profits. Stockholders expect to be paid **dividends,** a percentage return on their investment. But you also need to keep some of the profits as **retained earnings,** to be re-invested in the company to make it grow and expand. The stockholders also have an interest in some of the profits being plowed back into the company because they want to see the value of their stock *appreciate,* increase in value over time. Therefore, you and the board have a strategy decision to make.

KEY CONCEPT: DIVIDENDS ARE THAT PORTION OF CORPORATE PROFITS DISTRIBUTED TO STOCKHOLDERS.

KEY CONCEPT: RETAINED EARNINGS ARE THAT PORTION OF PROFITS RETAINED FOR REINVESTMENT IN THE CORPORATION FOR EXPANSION.

Normally, but not always, a well-run, prospering company will distribute part of its net earnings (above costs) as dividends and retain part for reinvestment. For example, let's assume that your company has earned a $10,000 profit over the past year, and that you (as CEO) and the board have decided that it would be prudent to retain half of it ($5,000) as undistributed corporate profits for re-investment. The other half ($5,000) is to be distributed to shareholders as dividends. What will each shareholder receive?

Because there are 10,000 shares outstanding, a $5,000 distribution means each share of stock is paid $.50 per share (10,000/$5,000). That means an investor who owns 2,000 shares is paid $1,000 ($.50 × 2000) in dividends. Note also that as the owner of 50 percent of the company—with 5,000 shares, you also receive a dividend of $2,500 ($.50 × 5,000). This is in addition to any salary you receive as Chief Executive Officer, which is part of the company's operating expenses.

RECAP

What we have just seen here is a classic, albeit somewhat oversimplified, example of how capitalism works. You as an *entrepreneur* developed a new product, patented it, started your own company, incorporated it, invested part of your own money in it, issued and sold stock to raise the

Figure 2-1a, Marvel Comics annual report cover

Figure 2-1b, Marvel Comic Books annual report, inside page

additional *capital* you needed to get the company going. After the stock was sold you established a Board of Directors, which elected a Chairman. The board appointed you as Chief Executive Officer to manage the company and you retained 50 percent ownership. This was your original goal, and if the company is successful at producing and selling the new mousetraps you will also be successful. You have become a capitalist, an entrepreneur who has been able to combine the factors of production: land, labor, and capital with your managerial skills and your willingness to take a risk to start a new company—and you share in the profits. Of course, if the company had failed you would have shared—in a big way—in the losses. That's how capitalism works.

Interestingly, just because you have started a new company that seems to be successful, your problems are not over. In addition to dealing with the day-to-day managerial problems of running the company, and dealing with the Board of Directors and the stockholders, you have to deal with the **Securities and Exchange Commission** (SEC), the governmental agency that watches over publicly owned companies. That means, among other things, you have to file financial reports, including an annual report.

THE ANNUAL REPORT

You and the board will also need to prepare an annual report, which summarizes the prior year's operations, projects future developments, and provides a detailed statement of the company's financial position. This report must be presented at an annual meeting to which all stockholders are invited to attend. Those who can't attend personally will be asked to sign a *proxy,* giving their vote to another stockholder or, more likely, to a member of the Board of Directors who will vote in their interest should there be an important issue to be approved by the stockholders.

HOW TO READ FINANCIAL REPORTS

Every year, a publicly owned company is required to file with the **Securities and Exchange Commission** a detailed accounting of its financial condition, including information about key personnel and important changes in the company's business. Most investors don't see this report, a "10-K" report, but rather see the annual report, which the company mails to stockholders. The annual report is less detailed than the 10-K, but it contains key information, which is what most investors are looking for. Another key document is the form "10-Q," or quarterly report. This gives a summary

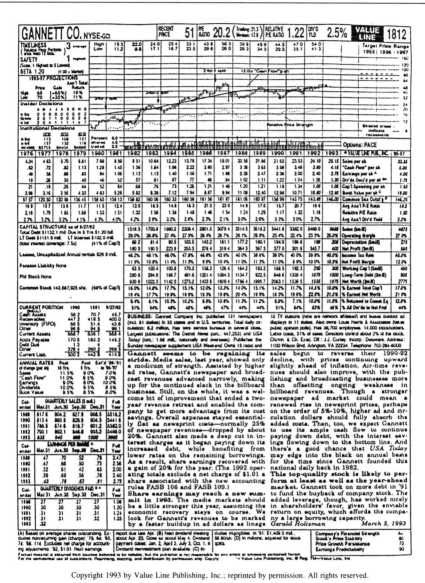

Figure 2-2, Value Line company summary

of a company's performance during its most recent quarter. Also, a form "8-K" must be filed with the SEC within 15 days of any events or changes in a business that are of great importance to shareholders. Many other documents must also be filed, but the 10-K, the 8-K, and the annual report are the most important.

KEY CONCEPT: THE SECURITIES AND EXCHANGE COMMISSION IS THE GOVERNMENTAL AGENCY CHARGED WITH OVERSEEING AND REGULATING THE FINANCIAL MARKETS.

Many libraries carry books that summarize financial information on companies that helps making comparisons among companies easy. For example, *Value Line Investment Survey* gives one-page summaries on thousands of companies and can be found in many libraries, or individual investors can subscribe. A sample company summary is shown in Figure 2-2.

The Income Statement

Probably the most important single figure we can find from financial documents is how much money the company we're analyzing is making or losing, the so-called "bottom line." It's called the bottom line because it is generally the last line in the first financial statement we'll look at, the **Income Statement.** Because a company's stock price is based on its ability to make money for investors in the future, and because an income statement records the company's historical record of making money, knowing your way around an income statement is crucial. An income statement is also one of the simplest financial statements to read, because it just takes all the money made during a certain period, and deducts the expenses required to make it. What's left over is either a profit (called net income or net earnings), or a loss.

KEY CONCEPT: A COMPANY'S INCOME STATEMENT COMPARES TOTAL INCOME TO TOTAL EXPENSES. THE DIFFERENCE BETWEEN THE TWO IS NET EARNINGS, OR NET PROFIT—THE SO-CALLED "BOTTOM LINE."

Suppose you're in college and you started a clothing business for students at your school. In a school year you sold $60,000 worth of custom printed sweatshirts, at an average price of $20 per shirt. You bought the shirts from a wholesaler for $10 each, then you paid a graphic artist to come up with designs, paid a printer to print the designs on the sweatshirts, paid friends to sell the shirts, and paid the bank interest on a loan you took out to buy the shirts initially.

In addition, as in the case we saw earlier, suppose you had raised money to start your business by selling stock. Let's say you kicked in $600 and a group of others kicked in $600, buying 600 shares you sold for $1 each. To find out how much money you would have made for each share, (called "earnings per share"), you simply divide the net earnings by the number of shares ($12,000/1,200 = $10). Does this mean that everyone who holds a share of stock gets paid $10? Not necessarily. As we have seen, the company can decide whether it wants to pay out some or all of the profits. This payout is the dividend. What's kept in the company are called retained earnings. Those retained earnings will be invested to help the company grow even larger.

Let's suppose that half of the net earnings will be paid out in dividends and see how that shows up on the income statement. Sweatshirt Inc.'s income statement is found in Table 2-1. This income statement illustrates how at the top of an income statement we put all the money we brought in. Then each line of expenses chips away at our pile of money until—hopefully—there is profit left by the bottom line. Typical expenses range from salaries paid to employees, to minor expenses such as the cost of stamps used to send letters and the cost of the paper used to write a letter. Also, advertising is an expense, as is the rent you pay for the offices where you conduct your business.

Table 2-1:

SWEATSHIRT INC., STATEMENT OF INCOME

Dec. 31, 1992

Sales	$60,000
Cost of goods sold	$35,000
Gross profit	$25,000
Selling, general and administrative expenses	$ 5,000
Interest expense	$ 2,000
Income taxes	$ 6,000
Net earnings	$12,000
Earnings per share	$ 10

KEY CONCEPT: EXPENSES ARE THE COST OF MATERIALS AND SERVICES USED UP IN THE COURSE OF GETTING REVENUE. ALSO CALLED THE "COST OF DOING BUSINESS."

By comparing income statements from year to year, and from company to company in the same industry, we can determine whether the company is improving steadily, erratically, or not at all. Say, for example, that our sweatshirt company had the same sales in the next year, but we paid more for advertising, so profits dropped. Obviously advertising didn't increase sales, so our new advertising campaign actually hurt our profits—a poor business decision. Likewise, if a company's expenses increase while sales remain the same, it could be the sign of poor management.

Using Ratios

To help summarize data about profitability, we can use ratios, which show relationships between sales, stock prices and earnings. For example, by dividing a company's net income by its sales, we get a measure of what percent of a company's sales ends up as profits, called **return on sales.**

KEY CONCEPT: RETURN ON SALES = NET INCOME/SALES.

To compare profits to a company's stock price, we divide earnings per share by price per share, called the **price/earnings ratio,** or simply P/E. If there are two companies in the business, Company A with earnings of $4 per share and a stock price of $40 per share, and Company B with earnings of $2 per share and a stock price of $14 per share, which would you buy? Using the price/earnings ratio as a guide, Company A has a P/E of 10 (40/4), while company B has a P/E of 7 (14/2). Therefore, Company B is *cheaper*, because it's earning you more money for your investment dollar than Company A. So it would seem that, all things being equal, you should buy company B. However, for example, if company B has a major lawsuit against it, or has just had its main factory destroyed by fire, or if something else has happened that would cause demand for its stock to drop, and therefore its price, it might not be such a bargain after all. This is why a company must be thoroughly investigated before investing in it. Price/ earnings ratios don't always tell the whole story. Also, different industries have different price and earnings structures, so P/E's are most useful comparing corporations in same line of business—apples-to-apples, as it were.

KEY CONCEPT: A PRICE-EARNINGS RATIO IS A COMPANY'S CURRENT STOCK PRICE DIVIDED BY ITS CURRENT ESTIMATED EARNINGS PER SHARE.

The Balance Sheet

Another major financial statement that all companies must prepare is the balance sheet. The balance sheet shows what a business owns, what a business owes and what's left over at a certain point in time. This differs from an income statement, which records the sales and expenses over a period of time. A balance sheet is divided into two parts, which, when added up, must be the same, or balance. A balance sheet can tell an investor a great deal about the financial health of the company. Is the company too far in debt? Does it have enough cash to pay its bills? These are important questions for investors.

KEY CONCEPT: A COMPANY'S BALANCE SHEET SHOWS WHAT IT OWNS COMPARED TO WHAT IT OWES.

In Table 2-2, the balance sheet of Sweatshirt Inc., we see that at the end of the year the company has $3,000 in the bank, is expecting to collect $2,000 from customers (accounts receivable), has $3,000 in unprinted sweatshirts and other supplies, and has a machine for putting designs on sweatshirts worth $2,000. Together, these make up the company's assets. On the other side of the balance sheet, the company owes the bank $2,000, and owes the sweatshirt supplier $1,988 (accounts payable). The company also has $6,000 in retained earnings—it made $12,000 in its first year, paid $6,000 out in dividends and kept the rest—and is recording the value of its

---

Table 2-2

SWEATSHIRT INC., BALANCE SHEET

Dec. 31, 1992

Assets		*Liabilities*	
Cash	$ 3,000	Notes payable	$ 2,000
Accounts receivable (money owed us)	$ 3,000	Accounts payable (money we owe)	$ 1,988
Supplies	$ 2,000	*Stockholder's equity*	
Embossing equipment	$ 2,000	Common stock	$ 12
	$10,000	Retained earnings	$ 6,000
			$ 6,012
		Total liabilities and stockholders equity:	$10,000

stock at $12. This doesn't reflect the true value of the stock, but is simply the stock recorded at par value, in this case a penny a share.

Debt Ratios

While examining a company's balance sheet, investors are often interested in the company's ability to pay its bills—its *current debt ratio*. This measure compares the company's current assets, or money readily available (cash, investments, accounts receivable) with current liabilities, or bills it must soon pay. This current ratio divides a company's current assets by its current liabilities. If a company has twice as much short term funds as it has short term bills—a current ratio of two—it is generally thought to have good bill paying ability. In Sweatshirt Inc.'s case, for example, it has $6,000 in current assets and about $4,000 in current liabilities, for a current debt ratio of 1.5 ($6,000/$4,000 = 1.5).

Another important ratio that uses balance sheet figures is the *equity ratio,* calculated by the total stockholders' equity divided by the company's total assets. This ratio measures the percentage of assets matched by stockholders' equity, and shows how much of the company's assets are financed by debt, as opposed to those owned outright by the company. Another way of saying this is how much "leverage" a company is using. **Financial leverage** is the degree to which a company borrows against its assets. Leverage is used to describe many different financial situations. In the most basic sense, leverage simply means using what you have to get more. It's important to remember, however, that using leverage almost always means adding some risk to a situation.

KEY CONCEPT: FINANCIAL LEVERAGE IS HOW MUCH A
COMPANY IS BORROWING IN RELATION TO ITS EQUITY.

The more a company has borrowed to get its assets, the more interest expense it has to pay and the greater the chance it wouldn't be able to pay its debts and would go out of business if earnings declined. But usually a prudent amount of debt adds to the earnings power of a company without significantly increasing risk, if it is invested properly.

Another measure of leverage is a company's *debt ratio,* or total assets divided by total liabilities. The higher the debt ratio, the more money a company has borrowed relative to its assets. In the best case, a company makes a higher return investing the money it borrowed versus the interest it must pay on the money borrowed. For example, if a company earns 25 percent on the assets it has, and can borrow money at 10 percent, it makes 15 percent on the money it borrows. Note, however, that highly leveraged companies represent higher risk to investors, and smart investors take this factor into account.

Other popular ratios use figures from both the income statement and balance sheet. *Return on assets* (ROA) is calculated by dividing net income by assets, and shows how efficiently a company uses its assets. Take, for example, two companies in the same industry. If Company A has a ROA of 15, and Company B has a ROA of 5, we know that Company A squeezes three times more profits out of its assets as Company B. A similar ratio is *return on stockholders' equity*, which divides net income by stockholders' equity.

All of these ratios, which can be calculated from a company's income statement and balance sheet, are important measures of a company's financial health. At the least they provide company analysts and potential investors with useful information to assess a company as a potential investment opportunity.

A CASE STUDY: PAYCHEX, INC.

Now that we've had an introduction to some financial statements, where to get them, and how to analyze them, let's take a look at a real company's financial statements, those of Paychex Inc., a service company headquartered in Rochester, New York. Firms across the country hire Paychex to process employee payrolls. Paychex also handles the taxes firms must withhold from salaries, and provides other services to firms either more cheaply or more conveniently than those firms could do themselves.

As you can see in Table 2-3, Paychex has shown a generally steady trend in increasing revenues and net income over this period. If we chart the net income against the company's

Table 2-3

PAYCHEX, INC. PRICE/INCOME

(in thousands)

DATE	REVENUE	NET INCOME
1984	$ 31,691	$ 2,023
1985	$ 40,930	$ 2,982
1986	$ 50,704	$ 4,170
1987	$ 63,891	$ 5,124
1988	$ 79,433	$ 6,935
1989	$101,154	$ 9,446
1990	$120,200	$ 8,566
1991	$137,081	$ 9,623
1992	$161,272	$13,702

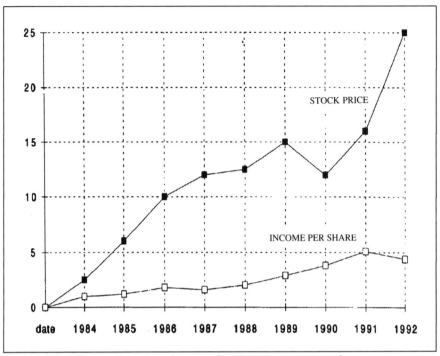

Figure 2-3, Paychex stock price, income per share.

stock price for the last ten years, shown in Figure 2-3, we can see that as net income grows, so grows the company's stock price. In fact, if you had bought $1,000 worth of Paychex stock in 1982, it would have been worth over $11,000 in 1992! By comparing the various expenses from year to year, we can see that the company is not letting expenses get out of control, but is staying very profitable even as it grows larger and larger.*

In Figure 2-4, we show the company's balance sheet for two years. This also reflects a very healthy company. The current assets divided by the current liabilities (current ratio) average around three, or much higher than our rule of thumb that two is a healthy ratio. Stockholders' equity is a very high percentage of total assets (equity ratio), showing that the company isn't relying much on borrowing for its assets.

WHO CARES ABOUT STOCK PRICES?

Interestingly, once a stock has been issued and the company has received the capital funds it needed for expansion or modernization, the

	Paychex, Inc.	
May 31		
(in thousands)	**1992**	1991
Assets		
Current Assets		
Cash and cash equivalents	**$ 5,215**	$ 451
Investments	**14,810**	10,586
Trade accounts receivable	**17,489**	15,644
Prepaid expenses	**2,024**	1,772
Other current assets	**2,083**	1,249
Total Current Assets	**41,621**	29,702
Property and Equipment *(Notes B & E)*		
Land and improvements	**2,564**	2,268
Buildings	**20,729**	19,970
Data processing equipment	**38,504**	29,650
Furniture, fixtures and equipment	**19,312**	16,893
Leasehold improvements	**846**	927
	81,955	69,708
Less allowance for depreciation and amortization	**38,080**	29,670
Net Property and Equipment	**43,875**	40,038
Other Assets	**746**	673
Total Assets	**$86,242**	$70,413
Liabilities and Stockholders' Equity		
Current Liabilities		
Trade accounts payable	**$ 3,519**	$ 3,040
Accrued compensation and related items	**7,298**	5,807
Accrued income taxes	**252**	314
Other accrued expenses	**2,278**	936
Current portion of long-term debt *(Note B)*	**390**	384
Total Current Liabilities	**13,737**	10,481
Other Liabilities		
Long-term debt *(Note B)*	**1,634**	2,024
Unamortized lease incentives *(Note E)*	**1,770**	1,627
Deferred income taxes	**1,696**	1,790
Total Liabilities	**18,837**	15,922
Stockholders' Equity *(Note C)*		
Common Stock, $.01 par value, authorized 30,000,000 shares:		
Issued, 19,765,738 in 1992 and 13,063,816 in 1991	**198**	131
Additional capital	**11,756**	9,518
Retained earnings	**55,451**	44,842
	67,405	54,491
Total Liabilities and Stockholders' Equity	**$86,242**	$70,413

See notes to financial statements.

Figure 2-4, Paychex balance sheet.

market price of its stock doesn't follow the day-to-day operations of the company. Though over time, the company's stock price rises and falls with its success. This is what has led some to suggest that the stock market is nothing more than a giant casino where players gamble to win or lose without any connection to the real world of business or the economy.

This is in one sense true, in another not. To see why, let's consider the two kinds of stock purchases we have examined so far. In Chapter 1 we bought a small amount of stock in three large (fictitious) companies. Our purchase had virtually no effect on the price of the company's stock or on its fortunes. In effect we were just gambling in the stock market casino that the stocks would turn out to be a good investment from which we would make some money. As in a casino, we could also lose.

But in the example of Mickey Mousetrap, Inc. we saw earlier in this chapter, if we had bought some of the newly issued stock we were certainly gambling, but we were also investing in the company in a more direct way. We were providing the company with the new capital it needed to launch a new business which, among other things, helped a new product come into being and created new jobs. This is quite different from simply buying an existing "floating" stock.

All that aside, it is also important to recognize that investors are not the only ones who care about stock prices. The management of a corporation with outstanding stock also has an interest in what happens to the price of its stock. There are several reasons. One is that if a company's stock price is increasing, then the public *perceives* that it is doing well and it will be easier for it to raise additional funds if needed. Another reason managers care about stock prices is that in virtually all cases the managers of a corporation own a portion of the outstanding stock. Recall, for example, that as the CEO of Mickey Mousetrap, Inc. you own 50 percent of the outstanding stock. When the price of the stock increases the management gains as much or more than the other stockholders. Finally, managers have to answer to their stockholders. If the company is not doing well and its stock price is falling the stockholders may demand an explanation—if not new management.

LOOKING AHEAD

Now that we have learned how to buy stocks and how to keep track of our investments as well as something about how and why companies issue stock and the accounting involved we need to take a broader look at the financial markets. In the next chapter we take a brief look at the history of the financial markets, the stock exchanges and how they work, and other kinds of investment opportunities. That will set the stage for a detailed look at individual investment strategies.

Chapter 3

The Financial Markets

In this chapter we will examine how the financial markets in the United States started, how they have changed over time and how they work today. The two stock market crashes of the Twentieth Century and the reasons behind them will be explored. We'll also examine overseas stock markets, and bond and U.S. Treasury security markets. Finally, commodity futures markets and financial futures markets and how they work to help people reduce risk will be investigated. Throughout this chapter we'll learn how to use newspapers to follow these markets.

HISTORY OF THE MARKETS

The words "Wall Street" are potent with meaning. They represent the financial heart of the United States, and conjure up images of companies being bought and sold, hectic traders screaming to get the best prices for whatever it is they're buying and selling, fortunes being won and lost, billion-dollar deals being made and even a crystal ball that holds secrets to the economy.

Wall Street is an actual street in New York City, which has been adopted as the symbol of the financial community because it is where financial trading began in colonial America and where much of it remains today. But "Wall Street" is an umbrella term that covers several different stock exchanges, and the nationwide network of broker/dealers that is referred to as the over-the-counter market, though "over-the-computer" would be a more accurate description today. It also covers a number of regional stock exchanges and even other types of financial markets that we'll discuss in this chapter.

Before Wall Street became Wall Street, it was a path along a wall of mud and brush built by Dutch settlers on what is now the island of Manhattan to keep livestock in and Native Americans out. Wall Street is located near the southern tip of Manhattan, as shown in Figure 3-1. The path's location between the Hudson River trade on the west end and the East River docks' importing business on the other end made it a natural location for merchants trading goods. Furs and tobacco, for example, were bought and sold here, and deals to insure cargoes and speculate in land were struck. But it wouldn't be until almost 1800 that what we think of as stocks and bonds would be traded.

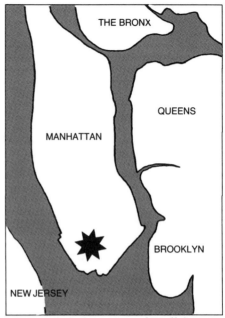

Figure 3-1, Location of Wall Street.

THE NEW YORK STOCK EXCHANGE

After the English took control of the region in 1664 the settlement became New York, which temporarily became the capital of the United States between 1785 and 1790. In fact, the first stock exchange in the young country was started in Philadelphia in 1790. But a year earlier, back in New York City where the first U.S. Congress was meeting—on Wall Street— Alexander Hamilton, the first Secretary of the Treasury, recommended that all the bonds that were sold to finance the Revolutionary War be backed by the federal government. At that point, the bonds weren't a terrifically popular investment, but when they received the backing they shot up in price. Shortly thereafter Hamilton sold stock to the public in the young country's first bank, the Bank of the United States. Thus the first securities started trading in the Wall Street area.

Securities brokers at this time were merchants and auctioneers who would meet informally to trade in a growing list of stocks and bonds, as well as the commodities that had always been bought and sold there. By 1792, the first **bull market** had begun, as demand pushed security prices higher and higher. Many securities, in fact, were traded like any other commodity, over a merchant's counter. This is where today's over-the-counter market gets its name. Merchants soon started scheduling stock and bond auctions, and finally a central auction at 22 Wall Street was started where securities were traded every day at noon. If you had a security you wanted to sell at that time, you would go down to the Stock Exchange Office, and give your securities to an auctioneer, who would sell the security to the highest bidder for a fee, or commission. If you had someone buy and sell securities for you (while you were conducting other business elsewhere) you also had to pay your agent, or broker, a commission. Some people, including auction members, who listened to the prices during the auction often got together after the formal trading was over to trade securities at reduced commissions.

KEY CONCEPT: A BULL MARKET IS WHEN SECURITIES
GENERALLY ARE INCREASING IN PRICE OVER A PERIOD OF
MONTHS OR YEARS AND TRADING AMONG THEM IS ACTIVE. IT
IS CONTRASTED WITH A BEAR MARKET, WHEN PRICES ARE
FALLING AND TRADING IS SLOWER.

Because this system was rather chaotic and disorganized, auction members met on March 21, 1791, to design an improved market that would better serve their own interests. On May 17, 1792, twenty-four men signed a document in which they agreed to trade securities only among themselves, to keep the same commission rates and to avoid other auctions. This agreement is called the *Buttonwood Tree Agreement* after a large tree at 68 Wall Street that securities traders used for shelter from the elements while trading. Thus the New York Stock Exchange was born. (The world's oldest exchange, the London Stock Exchange, had officially begun 19 years earlier.)

Under modern law, a group that agrees to fix prices and so control a market is called a *cartel,* which inhibits free trade and raises prices. So though the U.S. stock market is looked upon as the backbone of our capitalist system, ironically it started and continued for many years with distinctly un-capitalistic characteristics such as price fixing. Among other things, the Buttonwood Tree Agreement called for a fee of 0.25 percent to be paid on transactions.

In 1793 the exchange moved indoors. As business grew, the location changed several more times, until it finally settled at 11 Wall Street, where it remains to this day. On March 8, 1817, the members adopted a formal constitution, creating the New York Stock Exchange Board and establishing formal rules for their market. Every morning all the stocks to be auctioned were read to the seated board members who would then buy and sell the securities. The cost to be a member at the auction was $400. Today the price for a seat on the New York Stock Exchange is hundreds of thousands of dollars, and it is still referred to as a "seat," though no one sits while trading anymore.

THE AMERICAN STOCK EXCHANGE

By the middle of the 19th Century, the stock market was booming, in part because of the California gold rush in 1849 and because railroad stocks had pushed stock prices higher and higher. However, members of the New York Stock Exchange Board felt many of these shares were too risky to be traded. So nonmembers literally traded them in the street. By the 1870s the corner of William and Beaver streets in New York City was filled with these nonmember brokers, called "curbstone brokers," for obvious reasons.

When "the Curb" was expanded and moved to Broad Street, some brokers used offices in a nearby building from which telephone clerks took orders and yelled them down to brokers below. Hand signals, bright clothing and landmarks such as lamp posts where certain stocks were traded were used to help bring some order to the chaos. But adding to the confusion was the rain or snow storms that often pelted the market. Even though the market was outside, the exchange members were interested in presenting a proper image, and could be fined $10 for standing on a chair or fifty cents for knocking off a member's hat!

During the latter half of the 1800s, especially, the markets had little regulation, and were rife with corruption. Stock market manipulators tried— and often succeeded—to control prices of stocks through a variety of tactics. For example, manipulators often tried to make other investors believe a stock was trading fast and furious for higher and higher prices, when in fact no real trading was taking place. Once investors were sucked in, the manipulators sold their own stock at the inflated prices. Another tactic was to "corner the market" for a particular stock. By owning most of the shares, power could be influenced over the stock price in a number of ways, which would be illegal today.

In 1908, a leading curbstone broker, Emanuel S. Mendels Jr., organized the Curb Market Agency to develop trading rules for the market. However, the Agency had little power to enforce them. In 1911 Mendels and others drew up a constitution and formed the New York Curb Market Association, which eventually led to moving the Agency indoors on June 27, 1921. A parade of brokers singing "The Star-Spangled Banner" went into a newly finished building on Trinity Place behind Trinity Church. Inside, trading posts were marked by lamp posts resembling those left behind on the street. After another name change, this group became the American Stock Exchange in 1953, and is the second largest formal stock exchange in the country after the New York Stock Exchange.

Another key date in stock market history is May 1, 1975, when the fixed-commission rates dating back to the Buttonwood Tree Agreement were prohibited. As expected, commission rates soon fell, and now customers are free to negotiate commissions with brokers.

The Crashes of 1929 and 1987

During the 20th Century, the stock market has seen two serious crashes—dramatic drops in stock prices. One was in 1929. It foreshadowed the beginning of the Great Depression and brought to a close the wild bull market of the 1920s. The other, in 1987, was a much shorter-term decline that seemingly didn't signal much about the economy, but pointed out that the nature of the market had changed dramatically.

By 1929 the "Roaring Twenties" era of prosperity and a constantly rising stock market had brought unprecedented numbers of people into the stock market. Many of these people didn't buy their stocks with savings, but borrowed money to invest in the stock market. This borrowing, referred to as buying on margin, or **leverage,** increased the potential for gains, but also added to the risk for individual investors and the overall market.

KEY CONCEPT: LEVERAGE IS WHEN A RELATIVELY SMALL AMOUNT OF ASSETS IS USED TO CONTROL A MUCH LARGER AMOUNT OF ASSETS. OFTEN LEVERAGE INVOLVES BORROWED MONEY.

After World War I ended in 1918, the United States was the world's strongest and most prosperous country, and industry was booming. Record amounts of new stocks hit the market and were gobbled up by eager investors. Because the market was so inflated, when the bull market came to an end, the crash was spectacular. Starting on Oct. 23, 1929, the market started a quick downward spiral that wiped out $14 billion worth of paper wealth. On Black Tuesday, Oct. 29, 1929, the Dow-Jones Average lost 12.8 percent of its total value, which until 1987 was the greatest single-day percentage loss in its history. Over the next two to three years the market continued to sink, collapsing to one-fifth its size before the crash. Bank panics and factory closings were rampant and unemployment mushroomed. The Great Depression was underway. To bring some semblance of order to the situation, the Securities and Exchange Commission was formed in 1934 to eliminate manipulation in the market and administer rules to make securities markets and trading uniform and fair.

In 1987, another—less serious—market crash occurred. A number of factors came together to cause the October 19th "Black Monday" crash. A bull market that started in 1982 had pushed the Dow Jones Industrial Average up from 777 in August of 1982 to 2722 in August of 1987—a 250 percent increase. However, economic expansion wasn't the only thing pushing up stock prices. Big companies were being taken over by others—bought and sold for big profits, much of the buying and selling done with borrowed money. Bad economic news started shaking the market in the week before Black Monday. On Wednesday, Oct. 14, news that the country's trade deficit (the amount of goods we sell to other countries versus the amount we buy from other countries) had worsened. The federal budget deficit was getting worse and inflation fears were heating up.

The takeover business was being threatened by the House of Representatives Ways and Means committee, which was proposing that tax breaks which were key to making takeovers profitable would be cut. Prices of takeover stocks dipped. On Friday, October 16, the market made a record one-day drop of 106 points. Big institutions that trade huge blocks of stock using computerized "program trading" techniques were nervous*.

When the downward cycle continued Monday, many small investors got caught up in the panic and swamped brokers with sell orders. The Dow dropped 22.8 percent—508 points—and half a trillion dollars worth of stock market value was wiped out. However, unlike the 1929 crash, the economy was fundamentally sound. Stock prices bounced back 102 points the next day, and actually ended the year just slightly lower than they had begun. As a result, market reforms that would limit computerized program trading were enacted.

---

* Program trading involves the quick, computerized buying and selling of large amounts of stock and stock index futures—discussed later in this chapter. Such trading adds greatly to swings in the market.

REGIONAL EXCHANGES

In addition to the NYSE and AMEX, there are a number of regional stock exchanges in the United States. They include the Boston, Cincinnati, Midwest (Chicago), Pacific (Los Angeles and San Francisco), Philadelphia and Spokane exchanges. Specialists on the floor of all these exchanges use a special trading system to monitor prices on competing exchanges.

HOW STOCKS ARE TRADED

The way stocks actually trade hands and how prices are set varies depending on where and how many stocks are bought and sold. The New York Stock Exchange currently has 1,366 seats; the American Stock Exchange, 661. Once a seat is bought, it allows the owner to collect commissions for trading stocks and to participate directly in stock trading. While the floor of the stock exchange looks like pandemonium—and often is—everyone there has certain duties to perform and rules to follow.

For example, if you wanted to sell 2,000 shares of stock, you would contact the broker in your home town, who would immediately send the order to his firm, which has a seat on the exchange. From there the order goes to a broker on the floor of the stock exchange. With the order in hand, that broker goes to a booth on the floor, called a trading post, where that particular stock is traded. At that post is a specialist, whose job is to maintain an orderly market for the stock*. Each specialist has a list of a few dozen stocks for which he is responsible.

At this point, the broker with the order to sell your stocks finds out what the stock is currently trading for. Let's assume the specialist says the highest price anybody is willing to pay for the stock is $100.25 a share (the bid price), and the lowest price anybody is willing to sell at is $100.75 (the asked price). Now the auction begins. The broker won't automatically sell your stock at the $100.25 price, but will try to get a higher price, closer to the asked price. When he quotes a price someone is willing to buy for, another broker will yell "sold," and the transaction is completed.

If the trading post is surrounded by brokers looking to buy, and only a couple willing to sell, like at an auction where several people want the same item and keep topping each other's offers to try and get it, the price

---

* To assure that a stock can always be sold, specialists must also trade the stock out of their own accounts if no one else will.

falls. When a new price is set, a clerk enters the information into a device which shoots it out over the "ticker," a constant stream of security symbols and prices, which is flashed electronically on displays in brokerage houses and on computer screens across the world.

This auction process only applies to large blocks of stock, however. If you only want to sell or buy 100 shares, your brokerage firm routes them to the Designated Order Turnaround (DOT) system, a computer system that sends such orders automatically to the specialist's post. The specialist uses DOT to automatically buy and sell at the current bid or asked price. Most trades on the exchange run through the DOT system.

THE OVER THE COUNTER MARKET

A large and growing number of stocks and other securities not traded on exchanges are traded in the **over-the-counter market** (OTC) which is really a network of phones and computers that brokers use to trade stocks of more than 30,000 companies. OTC trading depends on market makers. These are securities dealers who stand ready to buy and sell certain securities at publicly quoted prices. A specialist on the floor of an exchange is a market maker, but in the over-the-counter system the role is filled by thousands of dealers. While historically most OTC stocks were small companies, today the OTC market boasts some of the biggest companies in the country—especially those in the computer and other high tech industries, such as Apple Computer and software giant Microsoft.

KEY CONCEPT: THE OVER-THE-COUNTER MARKET IS A MARKET
WHERE SECURITIES ARE TRADED OVER PHONES AND
COMPUTERS, RATHER THAN ON AN EXCHANGE FLOOR.

THE NASDAQ

Larger companies are traded on an advanced computer system that provides instant information on trading, called the National Association of Securities Dealer Automated Quotation system, or NASDAQ. About 5,000 companies' stocks are traded through this system. The National Association of Securities Dealers regulates the OTC market. To qualify to be listed on the NASDAQ, a company must meet certain eligibility requirements, including size, as measured by sales. The NASDAQ's tremendous growth in the 1980s has made it a rival to the New York Stock Exchange. Figure 3-3 shows how the exchanges stack up according to number of shares traded and dollar volume.

FOREIGN STOCK MARKETS

The rise of several overseas markets, especially the Tokyo Stock Exchange, has created more investment opportunities for everyone, and has helped make trading securities a 24-hour-a-day business. At midnight, when the U.S. securities market is closed and many people who work at it are asleep, trading is going on in Tokyo. Before dawn in New York City, the London Exchange has been alive for hours. Other key exchanges are located in Toronto, Canada; Frankfurt, Germany; Zurich, Switzerland; and Paris, France.

These days money, stocks and bonds are flowing more and more freely among the countries of the world. It is not unusual, for example, for a U.S. company seeking funds to borrow from a Japanese bank, or for a U.S. brokerage house to underwrite a stock offering in another country and sell shares to a third country. And when the U.S. economy is in a recession, another country might be in a bull market, providing good investment opportunities.

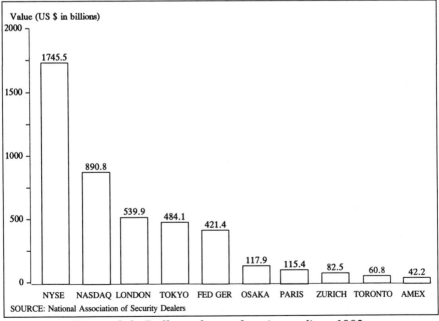

Figure 3-3, Dollar volume of equity trading, 1992.

Keep in mind, though, that no two countries are alike when it comes to trading securities.

For example, the London Stock Exchange didn't end its fixed brokerage commissions until 1986. As governments change through revolution or election, the new administration may take control of major companies, leaving stockholders hanging. Also, many countries don't make their companies provide the kind of detailed information to investors that the Securities and Exchange Commission does in the U.S. In addition, customs, politics and differences in currency add an extra layer of risk when investing in overseas companies. Figure 3-3 shows how the foreign exchanges compare to the U.S. exchanges.

PENNY STOCKS

If 30,000 stocks are traded on the OTC market, and only 5,000 are listed on the NASDAQ, what about the rest? These are traded on the so-called **"pink sheets,"** a daily list of all OTC market makers and their quotes published by the National Quotation Service. Until now we have been looking at stocks whose companies are closely followed by the financial community and are actively traded on the major exchanges or on the OTC market. All this attention brings a kind of security to these stocks, because the healthy competition for buying and selling keeps prices fair, or at least well-publicized.

But what about all those stocks traded on the OTC market which aren't actively traded and watched? Many of these fall into the category of **penny stock,** the riskiest type of stock. Because we are interested in risk and in how the stock market is supposed to work, we will examine penny stocks closely to determine what factors make them so risky. Typically, penny stocks are sold by young companies with little or no sales or earnings history. Often these companies are little more than an idea in an entrepreneur's head or just the foundations of a business. Those entrepreneurs are asking you to take a chance and fund their idea, with the hopes that if it takes off, you'll get in on the ground floor of a rising star.

KEY CONCEPT: PENNY STOCKS ARE STOCKS, ISSUED BY SMALL
NEW COMPANIES THAT DO NOT HAVE AN ESTABLISHED
RECORD.

Penny stocks are generally thought to have originated in Western gold and silver mines during the 1800s. Prospectors looking for seed capital sold stock, promising that if they struck the mother lode, investors would be rich. Denver and Salt Lake City are still centers for this type of stock trading.

Penny stocks generally sell for under $5 per share. Throughout their history, but especially in the 1970s and 1980s, penny stocks have also been associated with stock fraud and manipulation. In fact, the 1980s saw a proliferation of penny stock brokerage houses— from about 55 in 1984 to about 325 in 1989. Many of these firms were out to make a quick dollar from unwary investors, and this spread of fraud caused the Securities and Exchange Commission to write stiffer rules regarding the conduct of penny stock firms to help protect investors.

The market for penny stocks is no New York Stock Exchange, but government regulators estimated in the 1990s that $10 billion worth of penny stocks are traded each year. The North American Securities Administrators Association also estimated that in the 1990s penny stock investors were being bilked out of $2 billion per year! Of course, stock fraud can occur in any market, but why is it so easy in the penny stock arena? The reason is that a penny stock does not operate as we assume most stocks do. For example, a large company like General Motors is well-known, analyzed by millions of investors, subject to vigorous trading through many marketers. But, no healthy market for penny stocks really exists. Often little is really known about penny stock companies except what's in their prospectus, which, because the company has little or no history, is very thin. Little information, and a non-competitive market make for a highly risky situation with any security.

Take this scenario, which has happened thousands of times: A penny stock brokerage firm hooks up with an entrepreneur with an idea or a business. The brokers, sitting at banks of telephones with long lists of potential clients (called a sucker list) call up unsophisticated investors and make get-rich-quick promises about the future of the company, underscoring how cheap the stock is. Such an operation is called a boiler room because of the high pressure sales tactics used. "Just pennies a share!" the brokers say.

Usually this is misrepresentation because taken by itself, *a stock's price per share doesn't matter*. Think of a company like a pizza: you can cut a pizza into as many pieces as you'd like, but smaller pieces don't give you more pizza. The same is true with stocks. A stock represents a piece—a share—of a company, and if you have a million shares that represent one half of a company, or two shares that represent one half of a company, you still own half of the company.

In any case, when a penny stock issue is sold it starts trading and is listed on the pink sheets. Then in many cases unscrupulous brokers call a new wave of investors, getting them to buy the stock from the first investors, with the lure, "It's already gone up from 3 cents a share to 9 cents! Investors have tripled their money already." However, the price has only gone up because the brokers say it has. They sold it to the first round of investors at 3 cents; now they're selling it at 9 cents. A new wave of unsuspecting investors is taken in. The brokerage firm, meantime, is the only one buying or selling the stock, and is making a killing on the "spread" between the bid and the asked price. This spread on low priced stocks can be 100 percent of the bid price, or more, which means brokers can double their money on one sale.

A penny-stock brokerage house can only keep inflating a company's stock price for a limited time before the first earnings report comes out, then if it's not favorable, investors get wise to what's going on or regulators shut the firm down. Then the bubble bursts and a stock price can tumble to nothing overnight.

BOND MARKETS

To this point, we have concentrated our look at the financial markets on stocks, which are ownership or "equity" in companies. The other major type of financial securities is **bonds,** which simply represent money loaned to a company or government. Like other forms of debt, bonds have a limited life because they must eventually be repaid, while stocks exist as long as a company is in business. A bond holder typically gets interest payments over the life of the bond. At the end of the bond's life, typically 10, 20 or 30 years, the holder receives the original price of the bond, its face value.

KEY CONCEPT: BONDS ARE LONG-TERM SECURITIES ISSUED BY
CORPORATIONS AND GOVERNMENTS WHICH PAY A FIXED
INTEREST RATE AND ARE REPAID IN FULL AT MATURITY.

For example, if you buy a 10-year bond that pays 9 percent for $10,000 (the par value), you receive 9 percent interest payments every year on that par value ($900). At the end of the 10 years, you get the $10,000 back. The major difference is that while a stockholder hopes that stock prices will rise and to collect dividends, a bondholder collects steady interest payments over the life of the bond. But, bonds also rise and fall in price, and money can be made—or lost—by trading bonds, not just collecting interest. However, many investors hold bonds and other debt securities to collect the interest.

Bonds are usually issued by big institutions that need to borrow money. The biggest of these is the U.S. government which, through the U.S. Treasury, regularly holds sales of debt securities ranging in maturity from 3 months to 30 years. Similarly, many other countries issue bonds. Towns, cities, counties and states as well issue bonds to build schools, roads and other projects. Finally, corporations issue bonds for the same reasons they issue stocks—to raise money. And although bonds don't grow in value as the company grows, like stocks do, bondholders must receive their interest payments. Remember that dividends paid to stockholders are optional.

BOND PRICES AND RATINGS

Another difference between stocks and bonds is that once they are sold bond prices are only loosely connected to the health of the corporation or government that issued them, unless the institution experiences extreme financial difficulties. Instead, the main factor in the price of a bond is the interest rate it pays compared to what interest rates of other investments are paying at the same time.

This is an important question because it makes investing in bonds more risky than it might appear.

Let's take this example: Suppose a corporation sells you a $10,000 bond that pays an interest rate of 6.75 percent, or an annual return of $675 ($675/$10,000 = 6.75%). At the time it is issued, similar companies are also paying that rate. But now let's suppose that market interest rates in general rise to 8 percent. Would you still buy the same bond at 6.75 percent? Hardly, because you could get a higher rate somewhere else. Other investors feel the same way, so the value of your bond drops. In fact, your bond drops in value to the point where it yields the same rate of interest as the market is paying on newer bonds. If you wanted to sell your bond now, you'd have to lower the price to $8,000 to make its 6.75 percent yield equal to the market rate of interest of 8 percent ($675/$8,000 = 8%).

On the other hand, if interest rates fall lower than the rate your bond is paying, you can come out ahead if you decide to sell it. If the market interest rate falls to 5.5 percent then anyone who wants to buy your bond would have to pay a premium $12,000 to make it worth your while to sell it. In this case, the premium would make your $10,000 bond worth $12,000 ($675/$12,000 = 5.6%).

KEY CONCEPT: WHEN INTEREST RATES RISE, BOND PRICES
FALL. WHEN INTEREST RATES FALL, BOND PRICES RISE.

When you check bond prices in the newspaper, you'll notice that *both
the interest rate and the yield* are quoted. The yield is how much that bond
pays in annual interest divided by how much that bond is selling for at that
moment. The interest rate is a percentage of par value, which is the face
value of the security. In the example above, $10,000 would be the par value,
6.75 would be the interest rate. (See Figure 3-4 for details on how to read
a bond table.)

Another factor to consider in the bond market is the financial strength
of the company or government issuing the bond. If the company is in shaky
financial shape, it must pay a higher interest rate to get investors to buy its
bonds. If you buy such a bond—called a "junk bond"—you'll be getting
bigger interest payments, but you'll also bear the risk that the company will
get into financial trouble or "default" on the bond, that is, stop making interest payments. This could be a temporary situation, or might become perma-
nent if the company goes out of business, leaving the bonds worthless. The

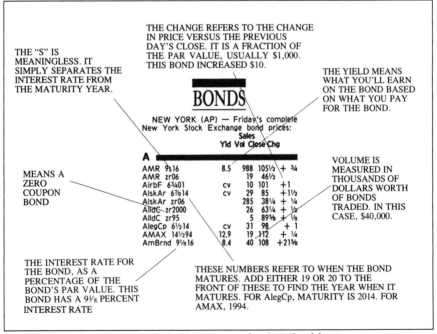

Figure 3-4, How to read a bond table.

degree of risk in bonds can be determined from ratings provided by bond companies, the best known of which are Standard & Poor's and Moody's. These companies have developed rating scales that make judging bond safety relatively simple. For example, a "triple A" bond rating means it is the highest quality and safest bond, while a "B" bond belongs to a company in financial trouble that probably won't be able to keep up interest payments. A "D" bond is in default.

Another risk of owning bonds is that many are "callable," meaning the issuer can buy them back from bondholders before they mature. You may say, "that's not so bad, I get my money back." But bonds are generally called when interest rates fall so much that the issuer can sell more bonds at lower interest rates, thus cutting back on the amount of interest paid. If a bond you own is called, you're stuck with reinvesting your money at lower interest rates than you were getting.

U.S. TREASURY BONDS

The U.S. Treasury sells several different kinds of debt. By tradition, Treasury securities with different maturities have different names. Short-term securities, with a maturity of one year or less are called Treasury *bills*. Those that mature in more than one year up to 10 years are called *notes*. Treasury securities that mature in 10 to 30 years are called *bonds*. Corporate bonds follow the same terminology. Because U.S. Treasury securities are backed by the U.S. government, they are considered the ultimate in safe investments. That safety, combined with the huge number of treasury bonds on the market (equalling $4.3 *trillion* in 1993), make them one of the most popular investments in the world. We'll learn more about investing in U.S. Treasury securities in the next chapter. (To see how to follow treasury bonds see Figure 3-5.)

Some federal government agencies also issue debt securities for various specific purposes. For example, the Government National Mortgage Association (nicknamed Ginnie Mae), buys mortgages from private lenders, bundles them together, and sells them as securities called Ginnie Maes. The association guarantees timely payment of principal and interest to Ginnie Mae bond holders.

How do you buy bonds? Just ask your broker. They are traded on stock exchanges or over-the-counter. Also treasury securities can be bought directly from the government through auctions held through the Federal Reserve Bank, which saves you brokers' commissions but involves some

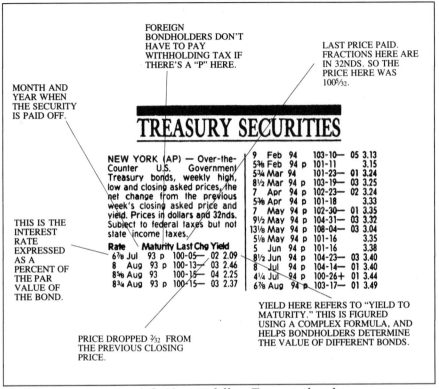

FOREIGN
BONDHOLDERS DON'T
HAVE TO PAY
WITHHOLDING TAX IF
THERE'S A "P" HERE.

LAST PRICE PAID.
FRACTIONS HERE ARE
IN 32NDS. SO THE
PRICE HERE WAS
100⁵/₃₂.

MONTH AND
YEAR WHEN
THE SECURITY
IS PAID OFF.

TREASURY SECURITIES

NEW YORK (AP) — Over-the-
Counter U.S. Government
Treasury bonds, weekly high,
low and closing asked prices, the
net change from the previous
week's closing asked price and
yield. Prices in dollars and 32nds.
Subject to federal taxes but not
state income taxes.

THIS IS THE
INTEREST
RATE
EXPRESSED
AS A
PERCENT OF
THE PAR
VALUE OF
THE BOND.

Rate	Maturity		Last	Chg	Yield
6⅞ Jul	93	p	100-05—	02	2.09
8 Aug	93	p	100-13—	03	2.46
8⅝ Aug	93		100-15—	04	2.25
8¾ Aug	93	p	100-15—	03	2.37

9 Feb	94		103-10—	05	3.13
5⅜ Feb	94	p	101-11		3.15
5¾ Mar	94		101-23—	01	3.24
8½ Mar	94	p	103-19—	03	3.25
7 Apr	94	p	102-23—	02	3.24
5⅜ Apr	94	p	101-18		3.33
7 May	94	p	102-30—	01	3.35
9½ May	94	p	104-31—	03	3.32
13⅛ May	94	p	108-04—	03	3.04
5⅛ May	94	p	101-16		3.35
5 Jun	94	p	101-16		3.38
8½ Jun	94	p	104-23—	03	3.40
8 Jul	94	p	104-14—	01	3.40
4¼ Jul	94	p	100-26+	01	3.44
6⅞ Aug	94	p	103-17—	01	3.49

PRICE DROPPED ²/₃₂ FROM
THE PREVIOUS CLOSING
PRICE.

YIELD HERE REFERS TO "YIELD TO
MATURITY." THIS IS FIGURED
USING A COMPLEX FORMULA, AND
HELPS BONDHOLDERS DETERMINE
THE VALUE OF DIFFERENT BONDS.

Figure 3-5, How to follow Treasury bonds.

time and paperwork. Or, you can buy them through bond mutual funds,
explained in the next chapter.

FUTURES MARKETS

Finally, in addition to the securities market, there is also a **futures
market** that plays an important role in the economy and that presents investment opportunities for savvy investors. The futures market is complicated
in the sense that prices are agreed to in the present for the delivery of something in the future. The two main types of futures are commodity futures
and financial futures. We'll look first at the commodity markets—the market
for raw materials such as cocoa for chocolate, gold for jewelry, and many
others. Every day in many newspapers you can find the prices being paid
for these commodities when they change hands between businesses on what

is called the cash market, or the spot market. Figure 3-6 shows an example of spot market prices.

KEY CONCEPT: A FUTURES MARKET ALLOWS INVESTORS TO BUY SOMETHING NOW FOR DELIVERY IN THE FUTURE AT AN AGREED-UPON PRICE. MONEY IS MADE OR LOST BASED ON THE DIFFERENCE BETWEEN THE AGREED-UPON PRICE AND THE "SPOT" OR CASH PRICE ON DAY OF DELIVERY.

But producers and buyers of commodities are not content to buy and sell at whatever price is available when goods come to market. This is because prices often change rapidly. To understand why this is important let's take a simplified example of a cocoa bean farmer and a candy maker.

If you are the farmer, months before your beans will be harvested you want to guarantee the price you'll receive when they are delivered. The reason is that you know if there's a huge harvest the supply will be greater than the demand, and the market price will drop. So you sell a futures contract to deliver 10 tons of beans at a certain price.

Who buys the contract? Perhaps a candy maker who needs to have 10 tons of beans in three months to make chocolate bars. The candy maker may be afraid that a typhoon will ruin most of the

Figure 3-6, Spot market prices.

cocoa bean crop, causing the supply to drop and the price to rise. So both the farmer and the candy maker have "hedged their bets" and guaranteed their price in the futures market.

The futures contract has allowed them to reduce their risk, and so plays an important role in keeping business running smoothly for both buyers and sellers of raw materials, called commodities. A tremendous variety of commodities are traded in the futures market. They range from food such as wheat, orange juice and pork bellies (bacon), to metals and minerals such as gold and oil. Through futures contracts, the effect of all the potential disasters that can happen between now and when a commodity is delivered is minimized. War in the Middle East could disrupt oil supplies. Disease and weather could hurt crops and livestock. Strikes by transportation workers or food processing workers could delay delivery of products. Examples of commodity futures contracts are shown in Figure 3-7.

If the hedgers use futures to guarantee prices and reduce risk, where does the risk go? To speculators. Speculators don't grow, raise, mine or refine any commodity. They simply buy and sell futures to make money, and in doing so accept the greatest risk of all the financial markets. Without speculators, the futures markets would not work as efficiently and the hedgers could not be able to reduce their risk. Suppose a speculator feels that the price of oranges will skyrocket because of a killer frost expected in Florida. By buying orange juice futures at a lower price, and selling them at a higher price after the frost hits, the speculator makes a profit.

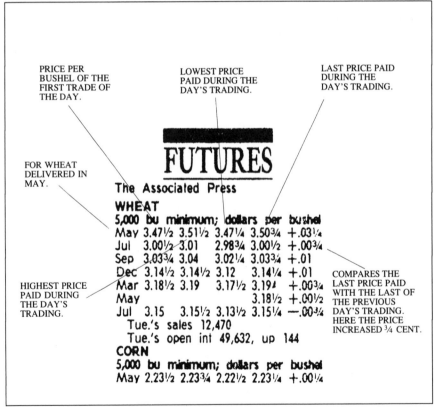

Figure 3-7, How to read commodity futures prices.

However, if the frost never arrives and oranges are plentiful, the price drops and the speculator gets squeezed—along with the oranges. Speculators make money in a variety of ways, ranging from predicting the impact the weather or political upheavals will have on commodity prices, to exploiting gaps—called spreads—between two contract prices.

In the same way commodities are traded on the futures market, so are stocks, bonds and currencies—the so-called financial futures.

Just as cocoa futures help the cocoa farmer and candy maker hedge their risks, so currency futures can help businesses engaged in importing and exporting hedge the risk of unexpected currency fluctuations. In the same way, if you are afraid of big swings in interest rates—say because you manage a portfolio of bonds whose value depends on interest rate changes—you can hedge your risk by buying Treasury bond futures. In fact, Treasury bond futures are the most commonly traded type of financial futures.

In the same way, you can hedge your stock portfolio in the financial futures market. What if you're afraid the stock market is going to fall sometime in the future? Or what if you think the market will rise? You can profit from such market fluctuations, or decrease your risk of holding stocks without actually buying stocks, through using *stock index futures*. These futures contracts are linked to the swings in value of broad market indexes, such as the Standard and Poor's 500. Unlike a commodities future contract, a stock market index doesn't require delivery of a portfolio of stocks when the contract expires—just the cash value of the contract. But like commodities futures, the price of stock index futures rises and falls depending on the gap between the day-to-day level of the index and the level set on the delivery day.

Begun in 1982, these futures are used primarily by large investors, such as mutual fund companies, insurance companies, and pension funds. Through many different techniques, stock index futures can reduce risk. For example, a portfolio manager afraid of a large drop in stock prices might buy a futures contract linked to the Standard & Poor's 500 Index. If the market does fall, the investor's portfolio of stocks also falls, but the value of the futures contract doesn't, thus offsetting the loss.

A popular method of using index futures is **arbitrage,** which means profiting from the differences in prices between the value of the futures contract and the actual value of the stocks that make up the index. By using computers and special programs, program traders can identify these gaps, very quickly buy the cheaper one in one market and sell the more expensive in the other market. They pocket the difference. Because the institutional

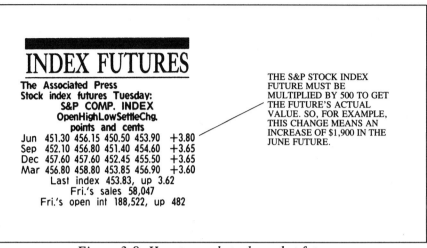

Figure 3-8, How to read stock market futures.

investors who use these computer programs buy or sell hundreds of millions of dollars worth of stocks very quickly, the overall volatility* of the stock market is increased. An example of stock index futures is shown in Figure 3-8.

KEY CONCEPT: ARBITRAGE IS PROFITING FROM THE DIFFERENCE IN PRICE BETWEEN THE SAME OR SIMILAR SECURITIES, CURRENCIES OR COMMODITIES SOLD IN DIFFERENT MARKETS.

LOOKING AHEAD

By now we have a good background in what makes the financial markets tick, and how to get started in investing. Next we'll look into different ways of investing. First, we'll start with the safer and easier investments, which include U.S. Treasury securities and mutual funds. Then we'll explore strategies for investing by picking our own stocks, and look at some strategies used by investment experts.

---

* Volatility is the market's tendency to rise or fall very rapidly.

Chapter 4

Investing the Easy Way

In this chapter, we learn about the different types of mutual funds and how mutual funds work. Then we learn about some very safe types of investments, and how we can set up our own portfolio of investments to match our desired degree of risk. Finally we explore some sample investment portfolios and some methods for investing efficiently.

INTRODUCTION

The answer to getting into the stock market with a minimum of cash and a maximum of safety is contained in two words: Mutual funds. Mutual funds are simply places where investors' money is pooled. Some mutual fund companies manage a fund that contains 200 stocks; other funds own many more. The fund may own hundreds of millions of dollars worth of stocks, but an investor can buy a piece of that fund for as little as $250. An average mutual fund share might cost about $10 to $30 each, so $250 will buy you 25 shares of a $10 per share fund. Mutual funds' share prices are simply the funds' worth broken into small units for convenience. The share price is determined by dividing the total worth of investments in the fund by the number of shares in the fund. This figure is called the *net asset value* (NAV). Net asset values are printed in newspaper mutual fund tables, and are a handy way to keep track of how your fund is doing. Mutual fund tables are relatively easy to read and understand. A typical one is shown in Figure 4-1.

There are a number of reasons to consider investing in mutual funds.

●**High returns.** The average equity mutual fund yielded about 13 percent for the 5-year period between 1988 and 1992, according to Morningstar Inc., a mutual fund rating agency. This is much higher than returns from many other types of investment, such as bank accounts, certificates of deposit or even U.S. government securities.

•**Greater diversification at less cost.** If you wanted to buy, say, stocks of 200 different companies on your own, it would cost many thousands of dollars. In fact, some investment experts estimate that to buy enough stocks to get a well-diversified (lower risk) portfolio today it would cost a minimum of $40,000.

•**Professional management.** Full-time financial professionals who use special research and complex investing techniques monitor each stock in the fund, and sell stocks or buy more when they determine the time is right. As an investor you don't have to worry about when to buy or sell stocks.

•**Tremendous ease of investing.** If you want to invest in a portfolio of 200 well-diversified stocks, just send a check for a few hundred dollars to a mutual fund company. When you want to cash it in, just request a check be sent to you.

DIVERSIFICATION

As we have seen, diversification is an important part of investment strategy. Remember how diversifying among Aardvark, Burp—Less and Caramba gave us an overall gain even though one of the stocks, Caramba, lost value during the time we owned it? Let's take another look at exactly how diversification works to decrease risk while still maximizing returns. Let us assume we take two stocks, ABC Co. and XYZ Co., whose prices have staggered according to the pattern

MUTUAL FUNDS

NEW YORK (AP) —The following quotations, from the National Association of Securities Dealers, Inc., are the prices at which these securities could have been sold (net asset value) or bought (value plus sales charge) Monday.

	Sell	Buy	Chg.
AAL Mutual:			
Bond p	10.62	11.15+	.01
CaGr p	15.00	15.75+	.05
MuBd p	11.01	11.56	
AARP Invst:			
CaGr	33.36	NL+	.09
GiniM	16.07	NL—	.04
Gthinc	31.06	NL—	.06
HQ Bd	16.63	NL	
TxFBd	18.33	NL	
ABT Funds:			
Emrg p	13.11	13.76+	.05
FL HI	10.41	10.93	
FL TF	11.29	11.85+	.01
Gthin p	10.86	11.40—	.01
Utilln p	13.77	14.46—	.02
AHA Funds:			
Balan x	12.61	NL—	.09
Full	10.67	NL	
Lim	10.49	NL	
AIM Funds:			
AdiGv p	9.89	10.20	
Agrsv p	19.55	20.69	
Chart p	8.82	9.33+	.02
Const p	15.41	16.31+	.07
CvYld p	14.82	15.56—	.04
GoSc p	10.37	10.89+	.01
Grth p	11.77	12.46+	.06

Figure 4-1, Mutual fund tables.

shown in Figure 4-2. As the graphs show, when ABC is up, XYZ is down. But, if we combine the rates of return for both stocks, the end result would be the average rate of return shown in Figure 4-3.

Notice that the graph combining the two has smaller peaks and valleys than if each company is plotted separately. This shows that the average rate of return, and therefore the price of a portfolio containing both ABC Co. *and* XYZ Co. will be more stable, and therefore less risky, than ABC or XYZ alone. What mutual funds try to do by investing not in just two stocks, but in dozens or hundreds, is increase this diversification and smooth out risk, while achieving a reasonable rate of return.

Another way to think about this is to consider two companies, let's say one that makes suntan lotion and another makes umbrellas. When it rains, the umbrella maker prospers; when it's clear, people rush to buy suntan lotion. So Suntan Inc.'s stock rises when Umbrella Inc.'s falls. Owned separately, your investment will have ups and downs according to the whims of mother nature. Owned together, though, their fluctuations tend to cancel each other out. On a larger scale, a mutual fund manager may seek this type of diversification through buying stocks in two industries, one industry that contains stocks of companies that tend to increase while the stocks of the other industry might sometimes decrease. The end result is more stable average prices and rates of return.

In addition to this kind of diversification, consider the effect on a two-stock portfolio when one company goes out of business, and its stock price plummets to zero. The portfolio would be devastated. But if a portfolio contains 100 stocks, each with about one percent of the portfolio's total, a single company going bankrupt would only decrease the fund's share price by one percent.

How far can diversification go to stabilize the value of your investments? Only so far. Even after all the risk that diversification can bring is erased, some risk remains. For example, when interest rates rise, stock prices change. When inflation rises or falls, prices change. When people become more cautious about investing because of impending war, political change, or other reasons, prices change. And a lot of times that means prices of all stocks regardless of industries or other features, will rise or fall together for a period of time.

One final point about diversification: Just because all mutual funds are diversified, that doesn't mean all mutual funds carry the same low amount of volatility and risk. On the contrary. Depending on how a fund's managers invest, the volatility can vary greatly from fund to fund. As an investor, you

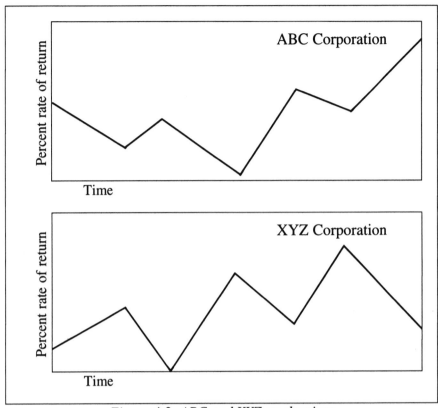

Figure 4-2, ABC and XYZ stock prices.

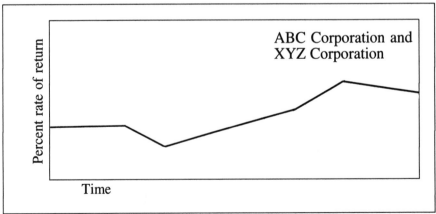

Figure 4-3, Average rate of ABC and XYZ stock prices.

need to look at a fund's volatility and returns over time, and decide whether that fund is right for you.

For example, let us consider two funds, both with excellent performance, as shown in Figure 4-4, which compares the returns of two funds. According to mutual fund rating firm Morningstar Inc., Financial Industrial Income Fund is considered to have below average risk, while Twentieth Century Ultra Investors Fund is considered to have high risk. As you can

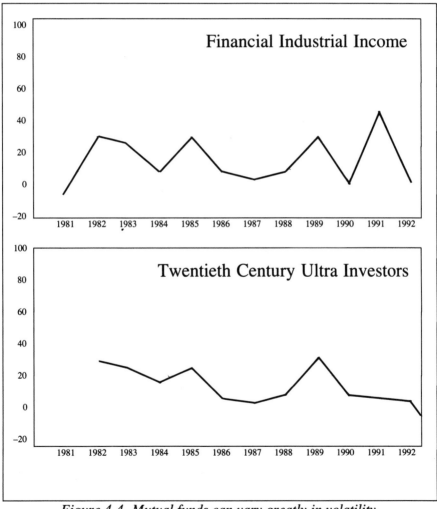

Figure 4-4, Mutual funds can vary greatly in volatility.

see, at times the two funds move closely together, but other times their returns vary quite a bit.

Mutual funds have grown tremendously in popularity over the past 15 years, as more and more investors recognize their benefits. In 1979, about $95 billion was invested in mutual funds. By the end of 1992, that number was $1.6 trillion—more than 17 times as much. The growth of mutual funds is illustrated in Figure 4-5 and Figure 4-6.

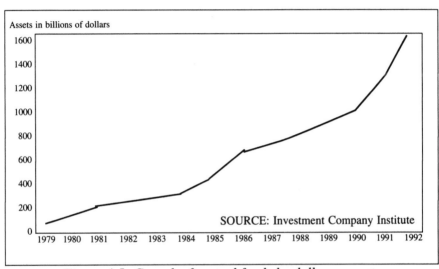

Figure 4-5, Growth of mutual funds by dollar amounts.

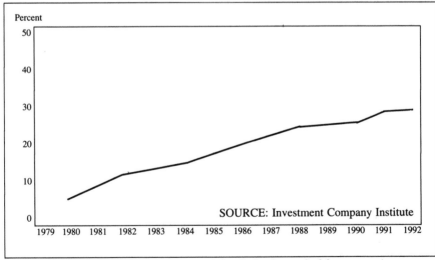

Figure 4-6, Growth of mutual funds by household penetration.

DIFFERENT TYPES OF MUTUAL FUNDS

Mutual funds come in a variety of different forms, each designed to meet different investors' needs. One fund's objective may be to pay the investor regular dividends; another may pay no dividends but try to increase share price as quickly as possible. So prudent investors will want to match their objectives with that of a particular fund. Also we can again use risk and diversification to analyze which mutual funds are best for us. There are five different basic types of mutual funds.

Equity Funds

Equity funds, as the name implies, invest only in stocks. But because there are so many different types of companies and investment strategies, this category contains a wide variety of funds. They range from high-risk, growth oriented funds to relatively stable funds that simply try to perform as well as the market does. Each is described briefly below.

●**Aggressive growth funds** seek to increase stock price, that is, to maximize appreciation, as their investment objective. They generally invest in stocks of smaller companies with high growth potential. They often also use risky investment strategies. Growth funds usually show the greatest volatility, but often the highest returns.

●**Global equity funds** invest in stocks all over the world, including in the United States. By investing internationally, diversification can be increased in two ways. First, more stocks to choose from means more and different investment opportunities. Second, all countries' economies don't expand and contract in unison. While Germany's economy may be going up, the U.S. economy may be going down, so Germany may provide better investment opportunities at certain times. However, with the benefits of overseas stocks comes an additional risk—that of exchange rates. Overseas stocks must be bought with the currency of the country where that stock is traded. And if the currency of that country rises or falls relative to the U.S. dollar, stocks in that country will become more, or less, expensive to U.S. investors.

●**Growth and income funds** invest mainly in companies whose stock prices are expected to increase at a healthy rate, and which pay dividends.

●**Income-equity funds** invest in companies with good dividend paying records. Especially key to these funds is the "yield," or the percentage of dividends paid per share price.

●**Index funds** try to match the performance of broadbased stock market averages, such as the Standard & Poor's 500.

●**International funds** invest strictly in non-U.S. companies.

●**Option/Income funds** invest in dividend-paying common stocks on which call options (explained further in Chapter 5) are traded. The objective is high current return.

●**Sector funds** invest only in stocks of certain industries or countries. Because these funds are limited in diversification, they often are more volatile than other funds. Examples are health care funds and biotechnology funds.

●**Socially conscious funds** choose companies according to their records of "ethical" responsibility. These funds may avoid companies that invest in South Africa, or are involved with tobacco and alcohol, nuclear energy or gambling, for example. But the government has no guidelines as to what is "ethical" business, so these funds' investment philosophies can vary a great deal.

Bond Funds

●**Corporate bond funds** usually invest only in corporate bonds. But some also invest in U.S. Treasury bonds, or other bonds issued by federal agencies.

●**Global bond funds** pick debt securities from countries around the world. Again, exchange rate risk is a factor.

●**Ginnie Mae funds.** Ginnie Mae is the nickname for the Government National Mortgage Association, which backs "mortgage securities." When people buy a house, they typically get funding in the form of a mortgage loan. Sometimes these mortgages are sold to Ginnie Mae through the institution that made the loan and then resold to investors. Ginnie Mae guarantees the loan's principal and interest will be paid on time, thus making mortgages more attractive to investors, who will then buy more Ginnie Mae bonds, making more money available for mortgages. Ginnie Mae funds are simply mutual funds that have most of their assets in such securities.

●**High yield bond funds** invest at least two-thirds of their portfolio in lower rated bonds, called junk bonds. A company with a low credit rating isn't in top financial shape, so to sell bonds, it must promise to pay a higher rate of interest to compensate investors for the higher risk of default on the bond. So high yield bond funds pay higher rates of interest, but carry greater risk.

●**Long-term municipal bond funds** invest in bonds issued by governments, including states, cities and towns. Generally governments borrow money through these bonds to build airports, roads, schools, etc. In most cases, income earned by these bonds is exempt from federal taxes. That means interest rates on municipal bonds are usually lower than those paid on corporate bonds because the tax advantages, in effect, boost the money an investor earns. For example, suppose you earned 10 percent on a $10,000 corporate bond investment, or $1,000. But you're in a 30 percent tax bracket, so you have to pay 30 percent of those $1,000 earnings, or $300, in taxes. You really earn only $700. So earning 7 percent on a municipal bond, and paying no taxes, or earning 10 percent on a corporate bond but paying taxes, leaves you with the same final earnings, $700.

●**State municipal bond funds** are funds containing bonds issued in just one state. If you live in that state, income from these bonds is free from both federal and state taxes—depending on your income level.

●**U.S. government income funds.** These funds can invest in U.S. Treasury bonds, Ginnie Maes and other government securities.

Mixed Funds

Mixed funds can use some combination of stocks, bonds or money market funds to achieve investment objectives. They include the following possible combinations.

●**Balanced funds** have three goals: To conserve principal (your initial investment), to generate income (through dividends and interest) and to provide long-term growth. To achieve this, balanced funds mix bonds, preferred stocks and common stocks. Preferred stocks get paid dividends before common stocks.

●**Flexible Portfolio funds** can be invested 100 percent in stocks or in bonds or in money market instruments, depending on what the fund managers feel is best.

●**Income mixed funds** use both stocks and bonds
to achieve a high level of current income for shareholders, through dividends and interest payments.

●**Convertible securities funds** invest in convertible securities, which start out as debt instruments—like preferred stocks—but can be converted into common stock by the investor. If managed properly, these funds can offer both dividend income and the chance to share in a company's growth. However, convertibles are generally not issued by large, strong companies, so they tend to be riskier than other securities.

Money Market Funds

Money market funds invest in short-term, high-grade securities such as Treasury bills, bank certificates of deposit and commercial paper—short-term debt issued by large U.S. corporations. They have the least risk of all the mutual funds because of the quality of securities required by regulators and because of the short life of the underlying securities—90 days or less. Some commercial paper may have a life of only a day or two. Money market funds always have a share price of $1, and so differ from stock and bond funds whose share prices rise and fall with the prices of their underlying securities. One of the most convenient aspects of money markets is that many offer check writing privileges, which makes them much like bank checking accounts that pay interest. Money market funds grow just like bank accounts.

The type of securities bought for money market funds determines their yields and levels of risk. Those investing in nothing but U.S. Treasury bills—considered the safest investment of all—have no risk. As fund managers mix in other investments, the risk of some part of the portfolio defaulting increases. Still, risk remains very low.

●**Tax-exempt money market funds** are just like regular money market funds, except they invest in securities of just one state, so interest is generally tax-free.

●**Precious metal funds** invest in gold, silver and other precious metals in a variety of ways.

Open-end Funds and Closed-end Funds

Finally, funds can be categorized as either open- or closed-end funds. Most mutual funds are open-end funds meaning the number of shares available is always changing, depending on how much money is invested in the fund. The price of the shares is determined by Net Asset Value, as we saw earlier. Closed-end funds are similar to their open-end cousins in that they can invest in stocks, bonds, overseas securities, and so on. However, closed-end funds raise money just once, and issue a limited number of shares, which are traded on stock exchanges just like regular stocks. Because closed-end funds are priced according to supply and demand—just like stocks—their share price can actually be above or below the price of the underlying securities.

For example, the price of a closed-end fund might be $16 per share, but its NAV—total value of securities divided by number of shares—is actually $18 per share. Therefore, it is trading at a price of 11 percent lower than its net asset value. Will this fund continue to trade at a discount? Will its share price continue to drop? Nobody knows, because buying closed-end funds requires the type of analysis reserved for buying individual stocks— which means they are not as straightforward to judge as regular mutual funds.

The demand for different types of funds is reflected in Figure 4-7, which shows that money market funds are the most popular mutual funds, reflecting people's desire for safety at a relatively high return rate compared to bank deposits. Next in popularity are bond income funds, followed by stock equity funds and tax exempt money market funds.

HOW TO EVALUATE MUTUAL FUNDS

With all these different funds to choose from, how do you choose which is best for you? There are three factors to take into consideration: *Performance, stability* and *costs*. Performance means how much shares increase or decrease in value over some period of time. Stability means how dependable are these returns. Do they swing far up one year, then down the next? Costs involve the question of how much the mutual fund company charges for its services.

Performance can be viewed in two ways. A fund's yield is how much income per share it pays to shareholders, made up from dividends and interest. That income can be reinvested in more shares, or paid directly to you.

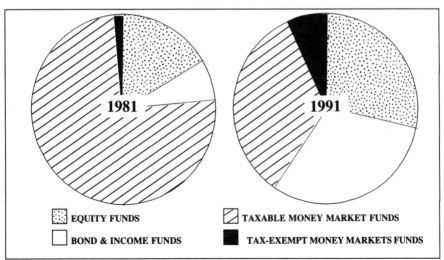

Figure 4-7, Distribution of total net assets, type of fund.

Yield is determined by dividing the income per share by the share price. A fund with a price of $20 per share and income of $2 per share has a yield of 10 percent. Yield is the key statistic when judging bond, income and money market funds. A fund's total return is its yield plus the change in the prices of the securities that make up the fund stocks, bonds, or whatever.

A variety of sources exist to find information on mutual fund performance, including magazines such as *Forbes, Money,* and *Consumer Reports*. Also a number of books can be purchased or checked out of your local library. A caution: *Be sure to read the fine print in ads for mutual funds* in newspapers and magazines. Some may claim to be the "highest performing," but mutual funds can be categorized in so many different ways that highest performing in a small category might not give the whole picture.

The most important rule to remember in judging performance is look at performance over a long period of time. Review at least five years, preferably even 10 years or longer. The reason is that any fund manager can have a lucky year or even several years. But how fund managers perform over many years of market swings is the true test of their reliability. Another important rule is consistency of management. If a fund has done well under one manager, and a new manager takes over, should you expect the same performance? Maybe, maybe not. Finally, fund size plays an important part of performance. When a fund gets so big that it can't trade securities quickly or efficiently, fund performance may suffer. Some funds limit their size for that reason.

A fund's stability refers to its degree of volatility, which is important to many investors who may have to cash in some of their shares within a year or two. *Forbes* magazine rates mutual fund performance in both rising and falling markets, allowing investors with different risk tolerances to find funds that suit them best. If you're investing over a long period, say because you're young and are saving for retirement, then stability shouldn't matter as much. Figure 4-8 is an example of a *Forbes* mutual fund chart.

Finally, a mutual fund's cost is important because costs can reduce the money you earn from investing in the fund. The most important of these costs is the "load," or the money—a sales commission, actually—that you pay to buy into a fund. The load is used to pay salespeople such as brokers or financial planners who sell funds. For example, if you invest $1,000 in a fund with a load of 5 percent, $50 is taken from your investment and paid to the salesperson, meaning you actually have invested $950, so your investment has to earn $50 just to break even.

However, a number of low-load (1 or 2 percent) and no-load funds

STOCK FUNDS
FUND SURVEY

Performance UP markets	DOWN markets	Fund/distributor	—Total return— Annual average 11/80 to 6/92	Last 12 months	Yield	Assets 6/30/92 ($mil)	% change 92 vs 91	Maximum sales charge	Annual expenses per $100
		Standard & Poor's 500 stock average	14.1%	13.4%	3.0%				
		Forbes stock fund composite	12.3%	14.0%	1.8%				$1.27
D	A	Aegon USA Growth/Aegon	13.0%	22.3%	1.5%	$44	15%	4.75%	*$1.37*
C	B	Affiliated Fund/Lord Abbett	13.6	16.3	3.9	3,623	7	5.75	*0.58*
A	C	AIM Equity–Charter Fund/AIM	13.2	12.2	2.0	1,058	439	5.50	*1.15*
A+	F	AIM Equity–Constellation/AIM	12.4	22.0	none	787	234	5.50	*1.20*
A+	D	AIM Equity–Weingarten Fund/AIM	15.1	11.0	0.4	4,451	168	5.50	*1.10*
C	C	AIM Growth Fund¹/AIM	10.8	7.6	0.9	163	−2	5.00	*1.21*
■ A	■ D	AIM Summit Fund/AIM	—*	13.6	1.4	504	27	**	0.75
		AIM Utilities Fund²/AIM	—*	19.6	4.9	97	33	5.00	*1.23*
		AIM Value Fund³/AIM	—*	22.9	0.8	176	60	5.00	*1.22*
		Alger Fund–Small Capitalization/Alger	—*	5.9	none	137	183	5.00b	*2.23*
		Alliance Counterpoint Fund/Alliance	—*	15.8	0.9	68	22	5.50	*1.64*
B	D	Alliance Fund-A/Alliance	10.9	15.0	0.9	708	5	5.50	*0.83*
D	D	Alliance Global–Small Cap-A/Alliance	7.0	5.7	none	66	−16	5.50	*2.28*
C	B	Alliance Growth & Income-A/Alliance	13.8	10.7	2.5	436	12	5.50	*1.16*
B	D	Alliance Quasar Fund-A/Alliance	11.8	3.4	none	280	−11	5.50	*1.64*
B	■ D	Alliance Technology Fund/Alliance	—*	15.2	none	144	−4	5.50	*1.71*
		Charles Allmon Trust/closed-end	—*	5.3	4.2	124	−3	NA	1.34
C	B	AmCap Fund/American Funds	13.7	13.9	1.3	2,678	22	5.75	*0.75*
B	A	American Capital Comstock/American Cap	14.4	13.8	2.3	905	4	8.50	0.82
C	A	American Capital Emerging Grow-A/American Cap	13.1	15.5	0.2	312	19	5.75	*1.14*
B	D	American Capital Enterprise-A/American Cap	10.3	14.3	1.3	680	13	5.75	*0.97*
D	B	American Capital Growth & Inc/American Cap	12.4	15.9	3.0	167	8	5.75	*1.14*
C	A	American Capital Pace Fund-A/American Cap	14.7	10.3	1.8	2,360	0	5.75	*1.01*
		American Gas Index Fund/Rushmore	—*	9.6	4.4	145	15	none	0.85a
F	A	American Growth Fund/American Growth	9.9	16.5	0.7	55	2	8.50	1.52
		American Heritage Fund/Amer Heritage	—*	40.0	32.3	28	NM	none	2.20
F	F	American Investors Growth/Amer Investors	−0.7	−3.3	none	49	−17	4.50	1.56a
D	A	American Leaders Fund/Federated	14.7	15.9	2.0	173	17	4.50	1.02a
D	A	American Mutual Fund/American Funds	15.0	12.5	4.1	4,464	14	5.75	*0.63*
C	C	American National Growth/Securities Mgmt	12.6	8.2	1.3	113	6	8.50	1.04
D	A+	American National Income/Securities Mgmt	14.4	13.2	2.8	104	24	8.50	1.23
		American Performance Equity/Winsbury	—*	6.4	1.7	92	48	4.00	*1.22a*
B	C	Amway Mutual Fund/Amway	10.8	6.3	0.1	52	10	3.00	1.10
F	A	Analytic Optioned Equity Fund/Analytic	10.7	8.3	2.7	88	−18	none	1.10
		API Trust–Growth/Amer Pension	—*	7.2	none	40	37	none	*1.97a*
		ASO Outlook Group Equity/Winsbury	—*	11.0	2.5	102	233	4.50	0.96a
A	F	Axe-Houghton Growth/USF&G	9.3	3.1	none	68	−13	5.75	*1.43*

■ Fund rated for two periods only; maximum allowable grade A. *Fund not in operation for full period. †Closed to new investors. §Distributor may impose redemption fee, with proceeds reverting to other fund shareholders. *Expense ratio is in italics if the fund has a shareholder-paid 12b-1 exceeding 0.1% pending or in force.* a: Net of absorption of expenses by fund sponsor. b: Includes back-end load that reverts to distributor. NA: Not applicable or not available. NM: Not meaningful. **Available only through monthly contractual plan. ¹Formerly Cigna Growth Fund. ²Formerly Cigna Utilities Fund. ³Formerly Cigna Value Fund.

SOURCE: Reprinted by permission of Forbes Magazine. ©Forbes, Inc., 1992.

Figure 4-8, Forbes *Magazine mutual fund charts.*

exist. These funds can be bought directly from the mutual fund companies. Interestingly, studies have shown that no great difference in performance exists between load and no-load funds. But if you can buy a fund with no load that has the same performance as a load fund, why pay a load? Loads are capped by law at 8.5 percent.

KEY CONCEPT: "LOAD" IS THE UP-FRONT FEE THAT IS PAID TO INVEST IN A MUTUAL FUND.

In addition to loads, mutual funds deduct a certain percent per year from the net asset value of the funds for administrative expenses. The lower this expense the better. Generally 1 percent or less is considered a low expense ratio, while more than 1.5 percent is considered high. One advantage of a large fund is that the mutual fund company can charge a lower percent and still cover its expenses.

Another annual cost is the so-called "12b-1" fee, named after the Securities and Exchange Commission regulation that allowed them. These fees are controversial because they are often overlooked by investors. They are used by mutual fund companies that don't have their own sales forces, and who can deduct 12b-1 fees to pay for advertising and marketing expenses.

Mutual funds can also charge a redemption fee, also called a "back-end" load, meaning you pay a percentage of your fund's value when you sell shares. Often, these fees decrease the longer you own a fund. For example, if you sell your shares after less than a year you may pay a 5 percent redemption fee. Selling in the second year you'd pay 4 percent, and so on until no fee is due after bout 5 years. Clearly, it is important to make sure you know all the fees and loads you will be paying before buying a fund.

WHICH FUNDS ARE BEST FOR YOU?

With more than 4,000 funds to choose from, how do you decide which funds are best for you? It all depends on your *investment objectives* and your *tolerance for risk*.

Do you want to save money for a big purchase in the future, such as sending your 3 year old to college or building a nest egg for retirement? Then growth funds may be your best bet. Growth funds during the 10 years before 1993 yielded more than 13 percent, on average. However, many funds have earned more than 15 percent on average over the same time period. Do you want a better rate than you're getting on the savings account at your bank? Then money market funds may be the ticket. Do you need a high amount of current income? Bond funds could be the way to go.

Table 4-1 shows the relative performance of the different types of funds for the 10-year period through April, 1993. As you can see, the average of the equity funds is less than the stock market itself as measured by the Standard & Poor's 500 index. In fact, most equity funds don't do as well as the S&P 500. So if you want to "beat the market" and who doesn't, be sure to pick a superior performing fund.

Most investors have a number of different goals, so they might buy several types of mutual funds. If you're investing for growth, say, why not invest in two or three funds, thereby giving yourself even more diversification. Should your portfolio have overseas stocks for global diversification? Buy an international fund or a global fund.

Once you have determined your goals and found several funds that meet those goals either by research in magazines, books or from recommendations by your broker or other financial professional, the next step is to get a mutual fund prospectus, as shown in Figure 4-9. A prospectus gives much more detail about a fund than any other source. As well as total return history and investment objectives, a prospectus lists how diversified a fund is, its risk factors, investment minimums, fees and expenses, investment strategies the managers use and restrictions on how the fund can invest. Once you have studied the prospectuses and decided which funds are right for you, simply fill out the application form and send in a check. Or have your broker do it.

RISK-FREE INVESTING

As we have said, all mutual funds with the exception of some money market mutual funds carry some degree of risk. But as you build your portfolio of investments, you will also be able to choose some "risk-free" investments such as commercial bank deposits, U.S. Treasury securities and money market mutual funds.

Almost all banks and savings and loans associations (commonly called "thrifts") carry deposit insurance from the federal government that guarantees deposits up to $100,000. Even when the savings and loan crisis struck in the 1980s and hundreds of thrifts closed, the federal government protected depositors, spending billions of dollars in the process. In a U.S. bank, money is very, very safe.

Banks offer a variety of ways to save, including the traditional passbook and statement savings accounts. Banks also offer NOW (negotiable order of withdrawal) accounts, which basically are checking accounts that pay interest. (These deposits have historically paid around a 5 percent return, though in recent years, as interest rates have dipped, they have paid significantly less.)

Certificates of deposit, or CDs, tie up your money for a specific period

---

Table 4-1

MUTUAL FUND RETURNS 1988-92

	5 YR. AVERAGE TOTAL RETURN		5 YR. AVERAGE TOTAL RETURN
EQUITY		Income	11.52
Aggressive Growth	13.33	World Bond	8.36
Equity-Income	12.16		
Growth	13.28	**TAXABLE FIXED-INCOME**	
Growth & Income	12.30	Corporate Bond—	
Small Company	13.81	General	10.35
International—		Corporate Bond—	
Europe Stock	4.20	High Quality	9.81
International—		Government Bond—	
Foreign Stock	6.62	Adjustable Rate Mtg	8.01
International—		Government Bond—	
Pacific Stock	4.91	General	9.66
International—		Government Bond—	
World Stock	7.63	Mortgage	10.01
Financial	21.70	Government Bond—	
Health	17.60	Treasury	11.09
Miscellaneous	15.13	Short-Term World Income	–8.46
Natural Resources	7.82		
Precious Metals	0.18	**TAX-FREE FIXED-INCOME**	
Technology	12.16	Municipal Bond—	
Utilities	14.61	Single State	9.58
HYBRID		**INDEXES**	
		S&P 500	14.76
Asset Allocation	9.97	Lehman Bros.	
Balanced	11.82	Govt./Corp. Bond Index	11.23
Convertible Bond	11.86	Lehman Bros.	
Corporate bond—		Corporate Bond Index	11.89
High Yield	10.16	U.S. Treasury Bills	6.03

SOURCE: Morningstar, Inc.

of time—generally from six months to five years. Cashing in early generally involves paying a small penalty in the form of lost interest. But CDs pay a guaranteed interest rate over a set time span, and come in several forms. You can buy them from your local bank (be sure to check interest rates at other banks, to guarantee you're getting the best deal), or you can buy them through a broker who can search the country from the best-paying CD rates. These "brokered CDs" can also be sold on a special market at no penalty, though the price you receive for the CD if you sell it will change as interest rates vary, just as with bonds.

FRANKLIN CUSTODIAN FUNDS, INC.

Growth Series, DynaTech Series, Utilities Series, Income Series, U.S. Government Securities Series

PROSPECTUS
FEBRUARY 1, 1993
as amended April 2, 1993

777 Mariners Island Blvd., P.O. Box 7777
San Mateo, CA 94403-7777   1-800/DIAL BEN

Franklin Custodian Funds, Inc. (the "Fund") is a diversified open-end management investment company consisting of the five separate series listed above (individually or collectively referred to as the "Series"). Each Series, in effect, represents a separate fund with its own investment objectives and policies with varying possibilities for income or capital appreciation and subject to varying market risks. Through the five different Series, the Fund attempts to satisfy a variety of investment objectives.

This Prospectus is intended to set forth in a clear and concise manner information about the Fund that a prospective investor should know before investing. After reading the Prospectus, it should be retained for future reference; it contains information about the purchase and sale of shares and other items which a prospective investor will find useful to have.

A Statement of Additional Information concerning the Fund, dated February 1, 1993, as may be amended from time to time, provides a further discussion of certain areas in this Prospectus and other matters which may be of interest to some investors. It has been filed with the Securities and Exchange Commission ("SEC") and is incorporated herein by reference. A copy is available without charge from the Fund or the Fund's principal underwriter, Franklin Distributors, Inc. ("Distributors") at the address or telephone number listed above.

This Prospectus is not an offering of the securities herein described in any state in which the offering is not authorized. No sales representative, dealer, or other person is authorized to give any information or make any representations other than those contained in this Prospectus. Further information may be obtained from the underwriter.

THESE SECURITIES HAVE NOT BEEN APPROVED OR DISAPPROVED BY THE SECURITIES AND EXCHANGE COMMISSION OR ANY STATE SECURITIES COMMISSION NOR HAS THE SECURITIES AND EXCHANGE COMMISSION OR ANY STATE SECURITIES COMMISSION PASSED UPON THE ACCURACY OR ADEQUACY OF THIS PROSPECTUS. ANY REPRESENTATION TO THE CONTRARY IS A CRIMINAL OFFENSE.

Figure 4-9, Mutual fund prospectus.

Banks also offer money market funds, which invest in the same type of funds money market mutual funds do. Bank money market funds tend to pay less than mutual funds, in part because of government restrictions on how bank money market funds are managed.

Investing in U.S. Treasury securities is also a common way to attain a risk-free return. The United States government issues three basic types of treasuries:

● **Treasury bills** are short-term securities with maturities of one year or less. The owner does not receive interest payments, but instead buys the bill for less than its face value; this spread is called the discount. The difference between the purchase price and the amount face value, which is paid at maturity, represents the interest on the bill.

● **Treasury notes** have a term of at least one year, but not more than 10 years. Unlike bills, notes have a stated interest rate and the owner receives interest payments twice a year.

● **Bonds** are essentially the same as notes, but have a term of more than 10 years.

● **Savings bonds** are perhaps the most familiar type of U.S. Treasury security to the average investor. They are sold in values anywhere from $50 to $10,000, and can be bought at banks or from brokers. Owners receive no interest payments, but buy the bonds at a discount to their face value; so you might buy a bond for $20 and collect its $50 face value when it matures in 10 years.

While investments in bank savings accounts and U.S. Treasury securities are in one sense "risk free," in another they are not. Clearly, the federal government won't stop insuring bank deposits or backing Treasury securities. That would, at the least, cause the financial markets to collapse. But, up until now, we have mainly spoken of risk in terms of volatility, the amount an investment's value rises or falls over time. However, consider inflation for a moment. And consider the risk of ignoring inflation in your investment plans.

If the inflation rate is 5 percent per year, and your bank is paying you 5 percent on a one-year certificate of deposit, the interest you can earn on the CD is canceled out. You'll still get paid the money owed you, but your investment won't be able to buy any more goods or services one year later. Its "purchasing power" is the same. You have merely kept up with inflation.

Also consider taxes. Using the example above, if your rate of return is 5 percent, the inflation rate is 5 percent, and you must pay 20 percent of your interest earnings in taxes, you have actually lost money in terms of actual purchasing power! Smart investors realize that they must combat the effect of inflation and taxes to make real gains in their portfolios. Figure 4-10 shows the effect of taxes on a portfolio, as compared to investing in a tax-deferred program, such as an Individual Retirement Account.

KEY CONCEPT: UNLESS YOUR INVESTMENTS ARE BEATING THE COSTS OF INFLATION AND TAXES, YOUR INVESTMENTS ARE NOT INCREASING IN VALUE.

BUILDING YOUR PORTFOLIO

Building your personal portfolio is much like grazing through a long buffet table. You can choose exactly what you want in exactly what proportions. You may leave the line with a plate of meat and potatoes (safe investments), or you may get a side order of something hot and spicy (individual stocks). It all depends on your tastes or your tolerance for risk. Say you had a $100 bill, and a friend said if you guessed the result of a coin toss (heads or tails) he'd give you $10 more. If you were wrong, you'd lose your money. Would you do it? Maybe if you really liked risk—or felt very lucky. Would you take the bet if the prize were another $100? Getting tempted? How about if the prize were $1,000?

The upward sloping line represents the risk/return relationship repre-

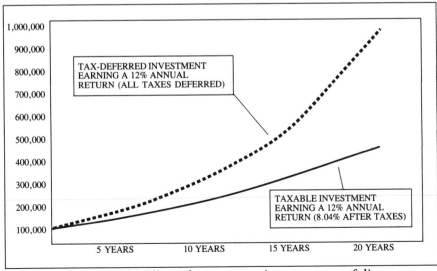

Figure 4-10, Effect of taxes on an investment portfolio.

sented by a diversified portfolio. We all have different levels of risk we're willing to take. One way to show these differences between people and investments is in Figure 4-11. At the 5 percent mark, let's say, is a risk-free rate of return. Investors are free to put all their money in treasury securities or bank products. However, the further you travel up the diagonal line, the more risk you take, and the higher return you expect. Investor A likes things nice and safe, and is happy with the risk-free rate of return. Investor B likes a little more risk—say a small investment in a growth and income fund, but with the majority of his money still kept in safe investments. Investor C has a higher risk, higher return portfolio, maybe consisting of growth stocks. Investor D is in trouble. He has all the risk of C, but not the high return.

One helpful device often used to illustrate risk in investments is the "risk pyramid." It shows the general increase in risk of different investments

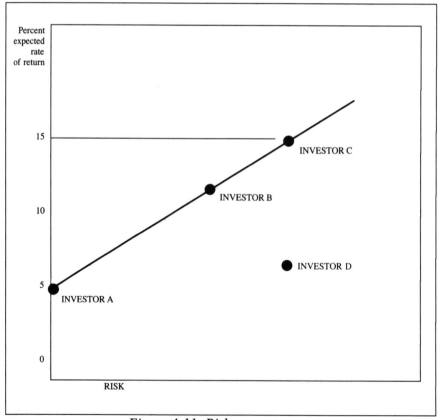

Figure 4-11, Risk versus return.

and is often accompanied by examples of portfolios that meet different risk levels. A risk pyramid is shown in Figure 4-12.

As a matter of strategy, if you are in your 20s and 30s and just starting to invest, you have many years ahead of you to ride out the ups and downs of the market. Therefore, financial experts often advise those just starting out to put a large percent of their investment capital in growth stocks. For

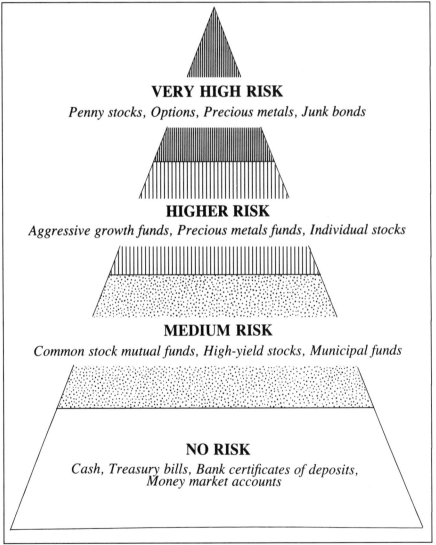

VERY HIGH RISK
Penny stocks, Options, Precious metals, Junk bonds

HIGHER RISK
Aggressive growth funds, Precious metals funds, Individual stocks

MEDIUM RISK
Common stock mutual funds, High-yield stocks, Municipal funds

NO RISK
Cash, Treasury bills, Bank certificates of deposits, Money market accounts

Figure 4-12, The risk pyramid.

example, Figure 4-13 shows some examples of higher risk, but high long-
term gain portfolios.

But, as you enter your forties, most financial advisors say you should
start switching money to less risky investments as you prepare your portfolio

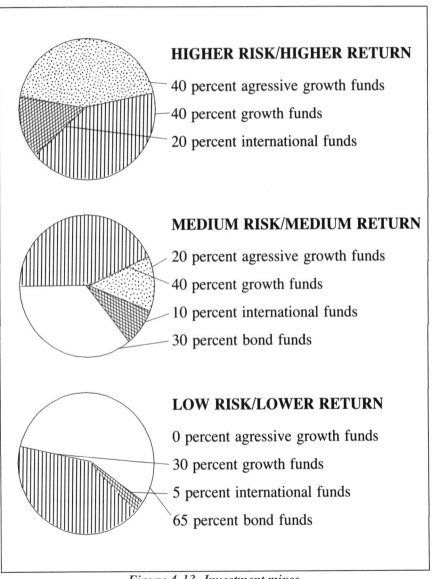

Figure 4-13, Investment mixes.

for retirement. Finally, as you enter retirement, you want to switch your investments mostly to ones that will guarantee steady income. Notice though, some money is kept in stocks to keep some growth potential in the portfolio.

INVESTMENT TIMING

When should you invest? Obviously, the best time to invest is when mutual fund or stock prices are low. How do we know low price points? The simple answer is, we don't. Experts in "market timing," or picking when to buy low and sell high, have dubious records of achievement. Plenty of people will sell you information about when you should buy and sell, but think a minute before buying. If they could really tell when to buy and sell, they'd be rich and they wouldn't need to sell you the information! They are much like those that hang around outside of race tracks who sell you information on which horses to bet on. If they really knew, they could afford to buy the race track and every horse in it with their winnings.

Fortunately, a method of investing called **"dollar cost averaging"** exists that assures you of buying more shares when the price is low than when the price is high. Dollar cost averaging simply means investing a certain amount of money at regular intervals. For example, every month you buy $100 worth of mutual fund XYZ. On the first month, the price is $10 a share, so you buy 10 shares. The second month, the price rises to $15 a share, so you spend $100 and buy 6.7 shares. In two months, you have spent $200 and bought 16.7 shares. Average price: about $12 per share. What if instead you decided to buy 10 shares a month, instead of investing $100 per month? The first month you would have spent $100 (10 × $10), and the second month you would have spent $150 (10 × $15). Total cost: $250. Price per share: $12.50—50 cents more than with dollar cost averaging.

KEY CONCEPT: DOLLAR COST AVERAGING GUARANTEES YOU WILL BUY MORE SHARES WHEN PRICES ARE LOWER, SO WHEN SHARE PRICES RISE, YOU'LL HAVE MORE SHARES ON WHICH TO MAKE A PROFIT.

If you don't have the discipline to write regular checks to your mutual fund, some mutual fund companies can help. By keeping a minimum amount in a money market account, some funds will automatically transfer funds from that account to a stock or bond fund.

INVESTING FOR THE LONG TERM

As we close this look at investing in mutual funds and building an investment portfolio, it may be worth emphasizing the benefits of investing in stocks and other securities, especially over a long term. Figure 4-14 shows the effect of investing $2,000 each year in a tax-sheltered retirement account, starting at age 21. (Our stock fund assumes a 14 percent average annual return.) At a fixed return of 7 percent, we make around $500,000 by retirement at age 65. At 14 percent, our investment of $2,000 a year over 44 years becomes over $4.5 million!

LOOKING AHEAD

In the following chapter we shift gears and take a look at a somewhat more complicated question: How to choose individual stocks and play the

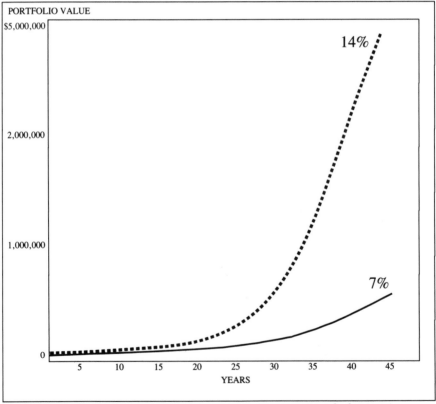

Figure 4-14, How the difference in returns is magnified over time.

market on your own. This is an entirely different issue from investing in mutual funds and letting someone else worry about the details of your investment. If you are going to play the market yourself keep two things in mind. One, *you need to know what you are doing*. And two, *be prepared to spend some time at it*. With those two *caveats* in mind you can make money in the stock market. You can also lose it.

Chapter 5

Investing The Hard Way: Managing Your Own Account

In this chapter, we will examine some methods for choosing stocks, including different types of stocks and different investment strategies. Some key traits of securities will be explained. We will also look at some of the more exotic types of investments and the risks that come with each of them. Choosing an investment professional will be discussed, as well as how to trade your securities.

INTRODUCTION

Now that we've explored the simple ways to invest in stocks and bonds—through mutual funds and following a broker's advice—it's time we take a look at making our own decisions and buying securities for ourselves. Knowing how to analyze stocks is a useful skill for many reasons. Buying and selling select stocks can add excitement and some real profits to your portfolio. It can help you understand more about economics and the world around you. Learning more investment language can make you more confident in many ways, from dealing with a broker to understanding the business section of newspapers better. And finally, either directly or indirectly, you will almost certainly own stocks or depend on stocks during your lifetime. Do you have a life insurance policy? Your insurance company invests in stocks. You may have a pension plan where you work. The pension fund invests in stocks. So the stock market affects almost all of us in one way or another. Realizing how stocks and the financial markets affect us also makes learning about securities more interesting.

DIFFERENT TYPES OF STOCKS

A stock can be a sleeper and a dog. It can even be a sleeper and a fallen angel. But it can't be a sleeper and a blue chip. What are we talking about? Labels investor give to stocks. Sometimes these labels are useful, and help us quickly understand the nature of a stock. For example, a dog is a stock in a worthless company. A sleeper is a stock that has greater value than its price would suggest, but hasn't been noticed yet by investors. We'll begin by looking at some stock categories to help us analyze stocks better, but first a warning: *All stereotypes are dangerous, and placing a stock in one category doesn't mean it will stay there forever.* In fact, many companies go through a cycle over their lives during which they may land in several different categories. Today's "high flier" may be tomorrow's "fallen angel." And some stocks could be considered in a couple of different categories at once. But determining which category a stock may fall into will help us decide whether that company is right for our personal portfolio.

Blue chip stocks. A blue chip stock is a stock of a nationally known company that not only continues to grow at a steady rate, but pays a steady dividend. The name "blue chip" comes from poker, where the most expensive chips are colored blue. Likewise, blue chip stocks are generally priced accordingly, with high prices compared to their earnings. They command high prices because of the steadiness and consistency of their performance. In other words, they are less risky, and investors are willing to pay more for this. Traditionally, blue chip stocks have included such well-known companies as International Business Machines, General Motors, McDonalds and Du Pont. The top blue chip stocks are sometimes called the "Nifty Fifty."

However, nothing lasts forever, especially in the stock market. IBM has long led the market in big computers, and became known worldwide as one of the best stock investments. In fact, it was nicknamed "Big Blue," as the bluest of the blue chip stocks. But as personal computers became more powerful, the demand for IBM's big computers fell, causing losses to mount. A radical restructuring of the company followed. Tens of thousands of employees left the company, and IBM's stock price plummeted, as shown in Figure 5-1.

Likewise, General Motors didn't move fast enough to improve its vehicles' quality and respond to the changing demands of consumers. Overseas competitors, especially from Japan, shook the foundations of General Motors—nicknamed "The General." In the 1980s and early 1990s, GM was closing plants and laying off large numbers of its work force. The lesson

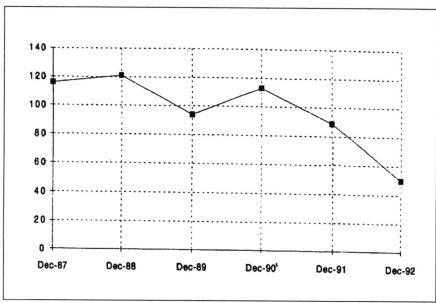

Figure 5-1, IBM stock price 1987–1992.

here? Smart investors don't invest in blue chips and then assume they'll be blue forever. Still, blue chips are generally considered the least risky stocks among the many options.

Secondary stocks. Not quite blue chips, these stocks also have stable businesses, but may not pay dividends as steadily, or grow as quickly as blue chips. A little more risky, but still proper for a conservative stock portfolio.

Growth stocks. These are stocks whose earnings are growing at a faster than average rate, and who reinvest all or most of their profits back in the business. If a company has a return on equity (net income divided by stockholders equity) of 15 percent per year, and doesn't pay any profits out in dividends, it will double its equity value in less than five years. Twice the equity may mean twice the profits and hopefully a doubling of today's stock prices. Figure 5-2 shows the effect of doubling and how to calculate it using the Rule of 72. Paychex, Inc., which we examined in Chapter 2, is an excellent example of a growth stock.

Keep in mind, however, that a growth stock is not necessarily a stock of a small company. Some large companies with billions of dollars in sales that keep plowing back most of their earnings into new plants, equipment,

A quick and easy way to judge an investment is to determine how quickly that investment will double, given its growth rate. And an easy way to figure how quickly something doubles is to use the rule of 72, which simply means dividing the number 72 by the annual return. So a 10 percent annual rate of return means an investment will double in 7.2 years (72/10 = 7.2). A 20 percent rate will double an investment in 3.6 years (72/20 = 3.6).

Doubling an investment's size is a powerful way to increase your wealth. For example, $1,000 doubled eight times is $256,000.

Especially when you're investing over a long time period, such as for retirement, getting a down payment for a house, saving for a child's education, think in terms of doubling when choosing your investment vehicle.

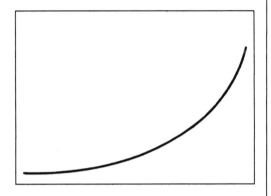

Figure 5-2, The rule of 72.

personnel, and so on, and keep making high annual returns are growth stocks, too.

Income stocks. Just as with income mutual funds, some stocks are valued highly for their dividends, and not what will happen to their price. For example, many utility companies (power companies and phone companies) serve a certain city, state or region and have a captive audience of customers. The business is, in many cases, a monopoly, so these companies can be depended on to earn steady profits, and pay steady dividends. Evaluating an income stock involves figuring out a stock's yield, (its dividends divided by the stock price), and comparing that yield to the yields of similar investments.

For example, if Amalgamated Power is selling for $10 a share, and it pays a $1 dividend, it yields 10 percent ($1/$10 = .10). Being a stock, however, there is always some risk involved, even though a utility is often a very stable business. Suppose Amalgamated's nuclear power plant is shut down for expensive repairs for two years, and the company is forced to buy power from somewhere else at a higher price? The dividend could be cut, and yield would drop. As a savvy investor, if you could get a bank certificate of deposit rate of 10 percent, you certainly would invest in a perfectly safe and stable CD versus a utility stock.

All income stocks are not utilities, however. A mature company in a mature industry that doesn't have great growth prospects may elect to pay its excess cash in dividends, instead of trying to diversify into other businesses with more growth potential. Again, yield is key for a stock of that type, which is sometimes called a "cash cow" (for all the money you can milk out of it.) Whether utility or not, companies that increase their dividends routinely are the best type of income stock.

Turnaround. Some companies have no dividends, or no earnings, or slumping sales. Or all three. And yet, these companies are highly prized by certain investors just because they are ignored by many investors who may not see the silver lining in their financial statements. A company in a slump may have lost its main customer, may have found that its main product causes cancer in lab rats, or may simply have been mismanaged to the point that it's on the verge of bankruptcy. Typically, these stocks' prices are very low, reflecting a pessimistic view of their future. However, an out-of-favor stock can turn around, often with dramatic results in the stock price.

For example, consider a company called Computer Consoles Inc., which was founded in 1968 and which made computers and communications equipment. Though it wasn't a household name, CCI had a good business for many years, including making the equipment that would "read" a phone number to you when you called directory assistance for help. CCI's stock was traded on the American Stock Exchange, and as the company grew in size over the years, its stock grew in value. By the early 1980s, CCI stock had hit about $40 per share, but there were clouds on the horizon. Competition from other computer firms was stiff. Net income dropped from $41.9 million in 1984 to $6.3 million the next year. The stock price dropped as low as $2.75 a share while the company hired new management that restructured the company. By 1988 the company had bounced back to the point it was an attractive acquisition target, and was bought by a British firm for $12.80 a share. Smart investors could have seen their investment increase 365 percent in less than a year, had they bought CCI before the acquisition.

Of course, some companies never turn around, and keep on dropping in sales, earnings and value until they go out of business. But if you believe bargains can be had in the stock market, many investors think troubled companies are where to find them, though the risks can be high.

FUNDAMENTAL ANALYSIS

Now that we understand the different types of stocks that are available, let's look at the several schools of thought in picking stocks. The most common and easy to understand is *fundamental analysis*. Fundamental analysts study the financial statements of a company, look at the company management, its business prospects, the industry in which it does business and other related factors to project the likely future performance of the company. Based on that prediction of future performance, a fundamental analyst determines whether the company's stock price is too high (overvalued) or too low (undervalued) in relation to similar stocks. Fundamental analysts buy bargains, or underpriced stocks, hoping that the market will recognize the hidden value in a stock, or hoping that the company will become more profitable, and have its price bid up accordingly.

One of the common tools of fundamental analysts is the **price-earnings ratio** (P/E), the measure of how "expensive" a stock price is related to the company's earnings. No single, useful average for the P/E exists for all companies, because companies can be categorized in so many different ways. However, we can judge something about a company by comparing its P/E to the overall market average—which itself often varies a lot. The market average for P/E often is around 15, meaning the average stock's price is 15 times its annual earnings per share at a certain period in time. The faster a company is expected to grow, the higher is its P/E. Often a hot computer or biotechnology firm will trade with a P/E of 25 or even higher. This means investors are willing to pay a premium for a fast-growing company. Likewise, if a company is in a business with a low-growth rate, it may trade at a low price-earnings ratio of 6 or 7.

KEY CONCEPT: A PRICE-EARNINGS RATIO IS A COMPANY'S
PRICE PER SHARE DIVIDED BY ITS EARNINGS PER SHARE.

Now suppose by analyzing a company, you determine that its growth rate will either soon increase, or will continue at a high pace, beyond what most analysts think it will. And this stock only trades at a P/E of 13, while companies with the kind of performance you're expecting this one will have are now trading with P/E's of 18. Your stock traded at $26 a share with earnings of $2 a share. (P/E of 13, or $26/$2 = 13). But you feel it should be trading at $36 a share (P/E of 18, or $36/$2). You'd buy this stock, and if your reading of the financial tea leaves turns out to be true, you'll see a big gain in your stock. If it isn't, you won't.

TECHNICAL ANALYSIS

While fundamental analysts believe that close scrutiny of financial data and other factors can predict future profits, **technical analysis** focuses on charts of stock prices and other data, and tries to profit from patterns discerned from charts. If the patterns indicate a future stock price rise, technical analysts buy; if they indicate a drop, they sell. To a true technical analyst (often called a chartist), details such as what the company makes, what its profits are and how its products are selling don't matter. All that matters is the psychology of the market, which they believe can be seen in statistical data like stock price and stock volume movements. One of the classic technical charts, called the "head-and-shoulders" pattern, is shown in Figure 5-3.

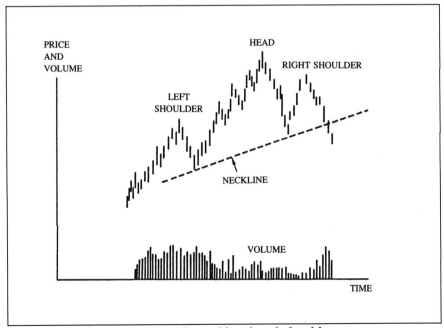

Figure 5-3, Hypothetical head-and-shoulders move.

Head and Shoulders

At the bottom of the chart the daily volume of trade of a stock is plotted. At the top are the high and low trading points for a stock's price during a day of trading. Working from left to right, we see that price generally increases day by day, and so does volume, showing a strong market tendency to bid the stock's price higher. Soon, however, a little dip is seen in price as some investors figure they've made a little money already, and want to cash in to make some profit. Then the next price rally occurs, culminating in the "head," but the volume is diminishing, indicating weakening support for the price. Finally, the stock price bounces up again on weak volume, and then starts to fall below the "neckline" with heavy volume, showing investors have turned negative on the stock, which is a clear sell signal.

Support and Resistance Levels

Another classic chartist's concept is that of "support" and "resistance" levels. If a stock trades within a certain (usually narrow) range for a long time, it is said to have support at the lower price, and resistance at the higher price. A support level is formed, the theory goes, because when investors see the stock price near the low, they figure it hasn't gone below that level in the recent past, and is likely to go up. So they buy. But when it rises near the resistance price, they also figure it can't go higher, so they'd better sell. When a stock price breaks through the resistance levels on high volume, it's a positive signal and a time to buy. Likewise, if a large number of shares traded push the price firmly below the support level, it's time to get out.

The Dow Theory

Probably the oldest and most respected of all technical theories is the **Dow Theory,** which applies not to individual stocks, but to the whole market. Charles H. Dow, a founder of Dow Jones & Company (publishers of *The Wall Street Journal*, among other things) believed that broad stock market movements predicted economic cycles. These days followers of the Dow Theory believe that three kinds of price movements exist, with the analogy often drawn to waves in the ocean.

KEY CONCEPT: THE DOW THEORY HOLDS THAT A BIG MOVE IN
THE STOCK MARKET IS SIGNALED BY THE DOW JONES
INDUSTRIAL AVERAGE AND THE DOW JONES TRANSPORTATION
AVERAGE REACHING NEW PEAKS OR TROUGHS.

"Primary" moves are seen as tidal changes, when the whole market generally moves up or down. These trends can last for several years, and foreshadow periods of recession (reflected in the market by bear markets) or growth in the overall economy (bull markets). "Secondary" moves are more like waves, and can occur over a couple months. They can temporarily wipe out the gains or losses of primary moves, but do not halt the overall bull or bear market. Finally, there are ripples, minor price changes, which are seen as meaningless. Dow theorists believe that when the Dow Jones Industrial Average and the Dow Jones Transportation Average both break through their previous peak points, a major new primary move may have started, and that is a good time to buy stocks.

The Contrarian School

Another school of technical thought is called contrarian investing, which could best be described as the "learn from the losers" strategy. Basically, contrarians find out what others are doing, because they believe that average investors with only a few dollars invested in the market don't know what they are doing. Measuring what small investors do is easily followed by the odd-lot statistics printed in most newspapers, as shown in Figure 5-4. An odd lot is simply a block of some stock under 100 shares.

Figure 5-4, Odd lot trading.

KEY CONCEPT: CONTRARIANS DO THE OPPOSITE OF WHATEVER MOST INVESTORS ARE DOING AT THE TIME.

Because small investors don't have a lot of money to invest (remember a round lot—100 shares—of a $50 stock would cost $5,000), they generally hold odd lots. So, according to this theory, when small investors are selling stocks, it's time to buy. When they're buying, it's time to sell. Does the odd-lot theory work? During certain periods, small investors have waited until the top to get caught up in a bull market bought high and then watched the bear drag down their stock prices However, the reverse has also been true. Odd lot traders sometimes accumulate shares in periods before bull markets.

Similarly, some contrarians look at mutual funds for their signal of what not to do. When mutual fund managers are leery of the market, and have a relatively large portion of their funds in cash instead of stocks, these contrarians think the time to buy is right. When mutual fund managers are completely invested in the market, it's time to sell.

Frivolous Technical Indicators

Finally, technical analysis can be carried to the extreme, as in the case of the Hemline indicator and the Superbowl indicator. The Hemline indicator holds that higher hemlines on women's skirts predict a bull market; lower ones a bear market. Shorter skirts in the 1920s and the 1960s predicted the bull markets of those decades, and the Great Depression of the 1930s was foreshadowed in 1927, when dresses lengthened.

Just as logical is the Superbowl theory, which holds that when an NFC team wins the Superbowl, the market will rally; when an AFC team wins, the market will sag. Generally this has been true, but not with a lot of certainty. In 1987, the year the NFC's New York Giants won, the market crashed. (See Figure 5-5 for a comparison of Superbowl winners and the market.) What these two theories show is that through sheer coincidence, a link sometimes exists between two unrelated events.

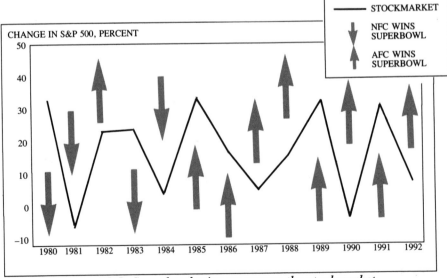

Figure 5-5, Superbowl winners versus the stockmarket.

TAKING A RANDOM WALK

What if the fundamentalists and the technicians didn't really know what they were doing? What if the pattern of trading didn't forecast the future? What if all securities were priced just where they were supposed to be, and price changes simply reflected information that popped up randomly and unpredictably, as information is apt to do? Who can predict a technology breakthrough that will strengthen one company and ruin another? Who can predict the death of a key executive? All of these things affect stock prices. In short, what if no way existed to foretell the future and "beat the market" over time? This idea, called the **Random Walk,** holds that if a blindfolded baboon threw darts at the stock pages, it could pick as good a portfolio as a room full of charts and the shrewdest fundamental analyst.

KEY CONCEPT: THE RANDOM WALK THEORY HOLDS THAT
STOCK PRICES FOLLOW A RANDOM PATTERN.

Under this notion, except for long-run trends—such as the truisms that the market will increase over time and that stocks of smaller companies will grow faster than stocks of bigger companies—*predicting price changes is impossible because prices follow a random pattern of change.* But, this theory holds water, ironically, only so long as a large number of technicians and fundamental analysts are constantly trying to "beat the market," and therefore bidding the price of stocks up or down according to new information. In other words, the Random Walk theory assumes that information about companies is quickly and efficiently reflected in their stock prices. Therefore it is also known as the Efficient Market Hypothesis.

Different versions of the Efficient Market Hypothesis exist, from that of the true believers, which assumes all information immediately shows up in stock prices, to more specialized versions. Such versions hold that people with inside information, such as company officers and their friends, can beat the market because they have special access to news that will affect a stock's price.

The Random Walk is a powerful idea, and many big investors practice it by trying to invest in stocks that mirror the major stock market averages. But to small investors, the Random Walk is comforting because it says that anyone can compete with the professionals if they buy and hold a diversified portfolio of stocks. Put another way, imagine the stock market as the ocean, and the higher the tide, the higher stock prices rise. You are standing on shore at low tide, and you watch as the waves come in and roll out. Will the next wave come in further than the last? No one knows. But over time the tide will come in, and you'll be waiting to reap the benefits.

GETTING SOPHISTICATED

Buying stocks is not necessarily a straightforward proposition such as buying a car. You could just call up your broker and have him or her buy what you want. But other ways exist for you to profit from stocks without actually owning them. In the rest of this section we'll explore some of these variations in investment strategy, and talk about how much to pay for stocks, and when to buy or sell them.

Warrants and Rights

Warrants and rights both give their holders the option of buying stock at a certain price by a certain point in time. When the stock is bought, the money goes to the company, just as with an initial public offering. Warrants and rights are considered another form of leverage, because they provide an opportunity to make more money based on what you already own.

Rights, called subscription rights, are given to shareholders of a company when their company is about to issue new stock. A right gives those current shareholders a short period of time (usually up to a month) to buy stock at a price lower than what the general public must pay. Shareholders can sell their rights, or exercise them.

A warrant is basically an option to buy a stock that is usually issued when a company sells bonds or stocks. However, the price at which the stock can be bought is set above what the stock is currently trading for. Warrants also differ from rights in the sense that they can last years, and in rare cases, forever. Warrants trade much like stocks. Figure 5-8 shows an example of a warrant in a stock table.

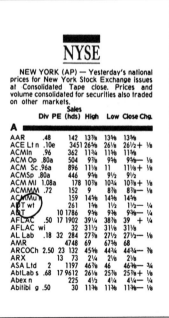

Figure 5-6, Warrant listings.

Warrants carry much more risk than stocks, but in certain circumstances can result in big rewards. Let's say that a company's stock currently trades for $5 a share, and it has issued warrants that entitle the holder to buy the stock at $8 a share. The warrant's only value at this point is the hope that the stock's price will exceed the $8 "exercise" price.

As an example, assume that expectations of future profits are worth twenty-five cents a warrant, and that's what the warrants sell for. Now the stock price starts to move, and the warrants pick up a little more value as the market price approaches the exercise (or call) price. Suddenly the stock shoots to $10. The warrants suddenly could be worth $2 (the difference between the call price and the market price) or more, if investors think the stock price is going to continue to rise.

If you hold the warrants, you can buy the stock at $8 a share, sell it for $10, and make a profit of $1.75 per share ($10 - $8 = $2, minus the $.25 price of the warrant). Now suppose the stock price drops back to $7 a share, $1 below the exercise price. The stock has decreased 30 percent from its $10 peak, and your warrants have dropped to . . . 12.5 cents! Because the stock price is going down, the market had valued them less at $7 than when the stock price was going up. Your $2 warrants have dropped 94 percent! Another factor influencing warrant prices is how close they are to expiration. The closer the expiration date, the less they are worth. Because of the quick potential for great loss or great gain, warrant buying and trading is not for the risk-averse investor.

Options

Stock options give a buyer the right to buy or sell 100 shares of a security at a certain price (called the strike price) before a certain date (the expiration date). Options usually last three, six or nine months. Unlike warrants, options aren't issued by a company, but are purely a product of the financial markets. Two basic kinds of options exist: *call options*, which gives the buyer the right to buy securities, and *put options*, which gives the buyer the right to sell the securities. A buyer of calls is hoping that the security's price will rise above the strike price before it expires, so the security can be bought at a cheaper price than the market price, then be sold at the higher market price and he can keep the difference as a profit (minus the cost of the option).

For example, suppose you expect the price of ABC Corp. will rise above its current $50 per share price, so you buy a call option that has a strike price of $55 per share. The price is $1 per share, or $100 to buy the option because they are bought in blocks of 100 shares. Then, as you expected, ABC rises to $65 per share! You exercise your option, buy 100 shares at $55, sell them at $65, and make a tidy $900. (You buy the stocks for $5,500, sell them for $6,500, and deduct $100 for the price of the option). That profit was earned with only a $100 investment.

The opposite situation occurs when a buyer of puts expects the price of a security to fall below the strike price. When this happens, the buyers purchase the securities at the lower price, then exercise their option to sell them at the higher price.

Most put and call options rarely are exercised. Why? Because the prices of puts and calls themselves rise and fall according to the stock prices. If a stock price is $10 above the strike price, and you have a call option that has risen in value to reflect that spread, you simply sell the option to make your profit.

All kinds of strategies exist for using puts and calls, which are generally employed by small investors. At one extreme, puts and calls can be said to limit losses in a portfolio, and so reduce risk. At the other extreme, options can be used to increase risk. For example, an investor can write "naked" calls, which means an option to buy stocks is sold on stocks the option writer *doesn't even own*. If the stock's price rises high enough, the writer could be caught having to buy securities at a high price, and sell them at a low "call" price. So, a good way of looking at options is that they transfer risk. When you buy an option, you are assuming risk, and for it, you expect a chance at substantial rewards. Again, options are a form of leverage. How to read the options tables is shown in Figure 5-7.

Selling Short

Selling short is another way of profiting when a stock price falls. Basically, a short seller borrows a block of stock, either from a broker or some other investor. The short seller then sells the stock, hoping that it will fall in price before the stock must be returned. If it does fall, the stock is bought back at the lower price, returned, and the short seller's profit is the difference between the two prices. If the price rises, however, the short seller will be stuck having to buy the stock back at a higher price to replace what he borrowed. A short seller can limit the loss by buying the stock before it rises too far, or buy buying a call option.

Buying on Margin

Buying stocks on margin is simply buying with borrowed money. To

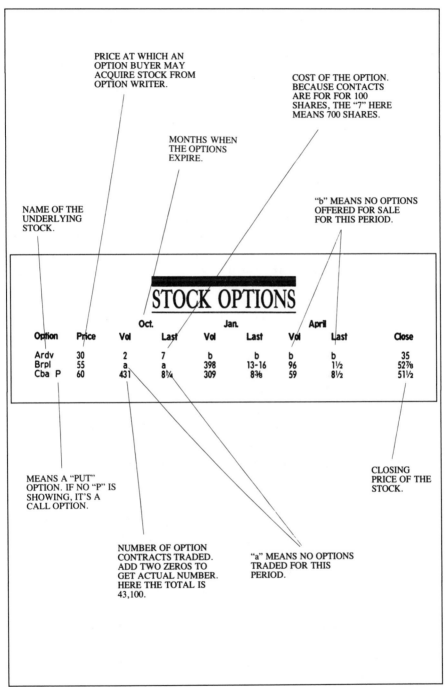

PRICE AT WHICH AN
OPTION BUYER MAY
ACQUIRE STOCK FROM
OPTION WRITER.

COST OF THE OPTION.
BECAUSE CONTACTS
ARE FOR FOR 100
SHARES, THE "7" HERE
MEANS 700 SHARES.

MONTHS WHEN
THE OPTIONS
EXPIRE.

"b" MEANS NO OPTIONS
OFFERED FOR SALE
FOR THIS PERIOD.

NAME OF THE
UNDERLYING
STOCK.

STOCK OPTIONS

Option	Price	Oct.		Jan.		April		
		Vol	Last	Vol	Last	Vol	Last	Close
Ardv	30	2	7	b	b	b	b	35
Brpl	55	a	a	398	13-16	96	1½	52⅞
Cba P	60	431	8¼	309	8⅜	59	8½	51½

CLOSING
PRICE OF THE
STOCK.

MEANS A "PUT"
OPTION. IF NO "P" IS
SHOWING, IT'S A
CALL OPTION.

NUMBER OF OPTION
CONTRACTS TRADED.
ADD TWO ZEROS TO
GET ACTUAL NUMBER.
HERE THE TOTAL IS
43,100.

"a" MEANS NO OPTIONS
TRADED FOR THIS
PERIOD.

Figure 5-7, How to read the options tables.

buy stocks on margin, an investor must have assets known as collateral—generally cash or qualifying securities—in a margin account with a broker. Currently, the margin requirement is 50 percent, meaning half of the total assets must be deposited by the investor. The other half can be borrowed from the brokerage firm for investment purposes. For example, if you put $10,000 in your margin account, you can borrow another $10,000 from the broker and invest it in securities. If you sink all $10,000 into one stock, and the price of that stock dips, you may have to either deposit more money in the account, or sell some of the stock.

Of course, the brokerage firm also charges interest on the money you borrow, and this must be taken into account. As we saw in the last chapter, borrowing money adds risk, and buying on margin is no exception. That borrowed money will magnify your gains, but also your losses. In other words, it will bring more volatility to your portfolio. Is this leverage? You bet. A margin account works much like when a company borrows money to increase its assets for financial leverage.

Stock Splits and Stock Dividends

As a stockholder, you need to be prepared for the day when the number of shares in your portfolio double or shrink, and the prices per share change radically overnight. But don't be alarmed, because stock splits and stock dividends usually don't change a thing about the value of your portfolio. A stock split usually occurs when a stock's price has risen to the point where the company feels it has grown too "expensive" for the average investor. Stock trading is done more cheaply in round lots (100 shares). By doubling the number of shares of stock on the market (splitting each share of stock into two shares, a 2-for-1 split), the price of a 100-share lot is cut in half. Of course, the price of the share is cut in half too.

Some investors get excited when they hear a stock is splitting, thinking it means more wealth. But remember the pizza analogy. A pizza cut into 12 slices isn't twice as much pizza as the same pie cut in 6 slices. Stock splits are sometimes thought to foreshadow good news by the company, such as an increase in the cash dividend. But studies offer questionable proof of this.

A stock dividend is much like a stock split, except instead of increasing the number of shares by 50 percent (a 3-for-2 split) or 100 percent (a 2-for-1 split), stockholders get another 10 percent or so worth of shares. Sometimes a company will do a reverse split, which almost always occurs when share price has dropped considerably, and the company wants its price per share to be higher to attract investors because low priced stocks are often linked with low-quality companies, such as penny stocks.

BUYING AND SELLING STOCKS

As we saw in Chapter 1, contracting a broker is one way to start your journey into the stock market. Choosing a broker who will also advise you on what to buy and when to sell is a very important consideration. You will want someone who is knowledgeable in the field, and who has a good reputation among other customers and brokers. Also you will want someone who understands the risk level you want to take, and how to get the highest return for the least risk. You need to know what strategies a broker likes to employ, and how they fit in with your own ideas about the market.

And always keep in mind that a broker makes money selling on commission. This means that every time you buy or sell a stock, bond or mutual fund, the broker makes money. Making sure a broker isn't moving you in and out of securities unnecessarily to make more commissions, a process called "churning," is something you must be mindful of. There are a couple alternatives to a full-service broker, who should provide you with investment advice, research and other literature. Discount brokers simply execute the trades you direct them to, and charge lower fees than full-service brokers. None of this is meant to imply that the vast majority of stockbrokers are not valuable financial advisors who will do their best to make your money work for you.

Financial planners are financial professionals who, at best, are trained in a broad spectrum of investments, and can advise you on all your financial needs, such as insurance, budgeting and investing. However, most financial planners also work on commission, so the same precautions hold as for full-service brokers. But again the vast majority provide advice and counsel that is well worth their charges. One alternative is "fee-based" financial planners who charge only for a financial plan, and do not make money from buying and selling financial products.

Finally, once your portfolio has increased past a certain point, you may want to hire a money manager. A money management firm is much like your own, personal mutual fund. Money managers offer full-time professional management, and are paid by taking a small percent of your assets each year as a management fee. You generally must invest at least $100,000 with a money manager, and often the minimum is half a million dollars or more. Many brokers can help you find a money manager, and can help you monitor that money manager's performance.

SOME MARKET LINGO

Finally, let us look at the financial terms for buying and selling stocks:

A **market order** tells your broker to buy or sell stocks at the best available price on the market at the time. The most common type of transaction, a market order generally gets you a price close to that quoted when you place the order with your broker.

A **limit order** is an order to buy at a certain price, or better. The **limit price** is simply the price set by the customer. For example, you might want a broker to sell a stock currently priced at $46 a share when it reaches $50. Or you might tell a broker to buy a stock currently trading at $33 if it falls to $30.

A **stop order** instructs the broker to buy or sell at the market price, once the security has hit a certain price, called the **stop price.** Stop orders are one way to limit your losses.

A **stop-limit order**, as the name implies, is a combination of a stop order and a limit order. It orders a broker to buy or sell at a certain price, or better, but only after a stop price has been reached.

LOOKING AHEAD

So now we have a good background in the financial markets, investments and investment strategy. In the next chapter we will step back and take a broad look at the financial markets, the economy and how the government's economic policy affects it. We'll also see how to use stock indexes and other easily available data to paint a clear picture of what's happening in the markets and the economy, and how that may affect your portfolio and your investment strategy.

Chapter 6:

The Stock Market and the Economy

Now that we have learned about the mechanics of the financial markets with some emphasis on investing in the stock market we need to take a broader look at the relationship between the stock market and the economy. (We're doing this to learn how to follow the economy and to understand what it is doing and where it is heading and how it affects the stock market.) This means we need to understand the indexes designed to track the stock market which, although useful, have some limitations. It also means we need to understand how the economy works and how the government influences it. Once we have accomplished that we will take a look at the various methods of forecasting the economy which, again, are useful but have some limitations.

THE MARKET INDEXES:
THE DOW-JONES INDUSTRIAL AVERAGE

There are at least 50 to 100 indexes designed to track various aspects of the financial markets. Some are relatively simple and easy to understand. The granddaddy of them all is the oft-quoted *Dow-Jones Industrial Average,* commonly known as "The Dow." The Dow is quoted on the evening television news every weekday and reported in virtually every newspaper daily. It is, in fact, so commonly quoted as an "average" that many people think the Dow represents the average price of all the stocks listed on the New York Stock Exchange. That's interesting because while the Dow is a useful barometer of what is happening in the stock market, it is not an average of anything, especially not of the "industrial" stocks listed on the exchange. As a measure of what is going on in the stock market or the economy in general it leaves a lot to be desired, but is still useful as an indicator of how the stock market is doing.

The Dow-Jones Industrial Average was first compiled in 1886 by Charles H. Dow, the co-founder of Dow Jones & Company and the first editor of *The Wall Street Journal*. Originally it was an average of the prices of 11 railroad stocks. By 1928 the Dow had been expanded to include 30 (mostly heavy industry) stocks.

The Dow is still compiled by the editors of *The Wall Street Journal* and the current list includes such diverse enterprises as McDonald's, Bethlehem Steel, IBM, and Philip Morris. So it's not limited to "industrial" stocks. The Dow isn't really an average either. Rather, it is computed by taking the sum of the daily closing prices of 30 selected blue-chip stocks and then dividing that figure by a number meant to take into account stock splits and other distortions.

So if the Dow Jones Industrial Average isn't based only on industrial stocks and it isn't really an average either, what is it? It's just an indicator of how things are going for 30 of the strongest corporations in the country (as shown in Table 6-1) whose stocks are traded on the New York Stock

Table 6-1
THE 30 DOW INDUSTRIAL AVERAGE STOCKS

STOCK	CLOSE, MAY 21, 1993	STOCK	CLOSE, MAY 21, 1993
Goodyear	$19½	United Technologies	$52
Allied Signal	$65½	Procter & Gamble	$50¼
AT&T	$60¼	Exxon	$64⅝
Coca-Cola	$41⅜	Chevron	$84¼
Bethlehem Steel	$20⅛	General Motors	$39¾
Sears	$53⅛	Merck	$38⅞
McDonald's	$50⅛	International Paper	$65⅞
Caterpillar	$68¾	ALCOA	$68¾
Disney	$41½	American Express	$28⅜
DuPont	$51⅞	Texaco	$64½
3M	$113⅝	Woolworth	$29⅝
General Electric	$93¼	Boeing	$40½
J.P. Morgan	$66¾	Philip Morris	$50⅞
Eastman Kodak	$52	Westinghouse	$15⅝
Dow average	**3500.03**	IBM	$49⅝

Exchange. Beyond that, it doesn't tell us very much, except that it's a quick indicator of market performance.

Much more meaningful are the broader indexes—discussed below—such as the New York Stock Exchange Composite Index, the Standard & Poor's index of 500 stocks, the NASDAQ over-the-counter index, and the Wilshire Index, which includes 5,000 selected stocks.

Therefore, most economists and market analysts feel it is a mistake to rely very heavily on the Dow to assess market conditions because it tends to be trader-driven instead of reflecting fundamentals, such as the performance of the U.S. economy. So why does the Dow continue to be considered one of the most important barometers of the market?

The best way to understand what is happening with the Dow is to look to the international sector. A large portion of the corporations that make up the Dow do most of their business internationally. Household names such as McDonald's, Coca-Cola, and Boeing can still do well even when the U.S. economy is in a slump. Exports to Japan and Western Europe are increasing rapidly. Coca-Cola does 80 percent of its business overseas, IBM 60 percent, and Boeing sells over 50 percent of its planes abroad.

Bad earnings reports may temporarily drag the Dow down or up each week, but the international tie-in seems to imply the Dow may not be as closely tied to the U.S. economy as was once thought. But the Dow still remains a useful indicator of overall market activity—so long as we remember it doesn't tell the whole story.

OTHER INDEXES

After the Dow, perhaps the second most commonly reported stock market index is the Standard & Poor's 500, called the "S & P 500." This index measures the performance of a broad-based selection of 500 stocks, which includes many of the stocks traded on the New York Stock Exchange and stocks listed on the American Exchange and over-the-counter stocks as well. Because these stocks are selected and weighted according to their relative values to reflect overall market performance, the S & P 500 is considered by many to be one of the more reliable indexes of market activity. Because of this, it is often used as a baseline by which to compare the performance of mutual funds and other financial institutions.

An even broader index is the Wilshire Equity Index Value, which measures the value of all of the stocks listed on the New York Stock Exchange, the American Exchange, and NASDAQ over-the-counter stocks as well. It

is by far the broadest and most accurate measure of overall stock market
activity and trends.

WHAT THE INDEXES TELL US

To be sure, the three popular indexes we have looked at and the many
more specialized indexes are useful in the sense that they give us a quick
reading as to how the stock market is performing. They tell us what the
financial markets are doing and how that compares to the historical record.
That, however, is all they tell us. What they don't tell us is where the market
is heading, nor do they illustrate how the market is going to affect the economy, or vice versa. Moreover, depending on your investment strategy and
the mix of your portfolio the indexes may or may not be of much value to
you as an individual investor.

For example, if you have invested heavily in blue-chip industrial stocks
the Dow may be an important indicator for you. But, if you have invested
in smaller growth-oriented stocks the Dow won't tell you much; instead you
will want to follow one of the more specialized indexes, such as the
NASDAQ Composite index, which tracks mostly small stocks. In either
case, however, you will want to have some idea of how the economy is
doing and where it is headed. The economy's direction will affect your stock
portfolio no matter what its composition—although in some instances not
by as much as you might think.

THE ECONOMIC INDICATORS

It is commonly thought that if the economy is doing well the stock
market should be doing well and if the economy is sluggish or faltering we
should expect the stock market to reflect that. Sometimes that is true; sometimes it is not. For example, in 1989 all of the indicators that are supposed
to—and usually do—predict the direction the economy is heading were
down, while the stock market was booming. This curious phenomenon par-
tially reflects the fact that once stocks are issued and traded in the market,
their value depends more on supply and demand than it does the underlying
economy;

In addition, there is a strong link between other forces in the financial
markets that determine interest rates, which is why many market analysts
believe that "interest rates are everything" when it comes to the stock mar-
ket.This means that interest rates are one of the most important indicators
to watch if you want to follow the relationship between the economy and

the market. When interest rates are low there are few, if any, options for investors other than the stock market. For example, in 1991 and 1992, when interest rates were at 30-year lows, many investors took their money out of low-yielding bank savings accounts and CDs and shifted them into the market directly or into mutual funds. This added demand was one reason the market continued to do well even though the economy was sluggish.

On the other hand, if interest rates are high then bank savings accounts become a more attractive investment and money flows out of the stock market. The smaller demand may depress stock prices even though the economy may be booming. All that means predicting the level of interest rates is one of the more important factors in predicting how the market may do at some time in the future. But, predicting interest rates means one has to be able to predict how the economy is going to do. Normally, when the economy is slow interest rates will be low; when the economy is booming interest rates tend to rise. That means an astute investor needs to have some idea of where the economy is heading. This brings us to the economy itself, and the question of how to understand it, follow it, and forecast the level of future economic activity.

WHAT MAKES THE ECONOMY TICK

Every nation's primary goal is to promote steady economic growth. Economic growth means that as more goods and services are produced the average level of income increases. That is, everyone can enjoy a higher average standard of living. The primary determinants of economic growth are: 1) technological change, 2) investment in capital, and 3) investment in human capital. Thus, a nation's productive capacity depends largely on its level of technology, its supply and quality of capital, and the skills of its labor force.

Technological advances improve the productivity of inputs—such as land, labor, and capital—and the quality of output, thereby increasing the rate of economic growth and raising living standards. Innovations—in the form of new products, machines, production techniques, and communication and transportation methods—also provide a powerful stimulus to economic growth.

Investment in physical capital is another major vehicle for increasing the rate of economic growth. Increases in the amount of physical capital available (such as tools and machinery) make the labor force more productive, since each worker has more and better capital to work with. Sustained high levels of investment should lead to higher productivity, higher wages, and a higher standard of living.

In addition to technological change and investment in physical capital, economic growth is determined by the level of investment in human capital. This includes the entire range of activities and programs related to a worker's health, training, and education. Indeed, recent studies have shown that investment in human capital may be the most important determinant of economic growth.

THE ROLE OF GOVERNMENT

Just after World War II, Congress passed the Employment Act of 1946, which charged the government with the following task:

The Congress hereby declares that it is the continuing responsibility of the Federal Government to use all practicable means possible . . . to promote maximum employment, production, and purchasing power.

But passing a law instructing the government to attempt to maintain full employment isn't quite enough to make that happen. Indeed, since the end of World War II the U.S. economy has experienced 11 recessions, some of which have resulted in unemployment rates of over 10 percent.

Recessions, in themselves, remain a bit of an enigma. It would seem, at first glance, that if the plants, equipment, and technical know-how to run them exist, and if trained people are able and willing to work, then keeping the economy running full tilt should be a relatively simple task. But the world doesn't work that way, for reasons that will occupy our attention throughout the rest of this chapter.

MONETARY POLICY

In its simplest version governmental economic policy is relatively easy to understand. Partly it involves monetary policy and partly fiscal policy. Monetary policy is controlled by the Federal Reserve, commonly called "the Fed." The Federal Reserve system is a quasi-governmental agency, which is the United States central bank. The Fed has control of the level of interest rates. The Fed is charged with supplying the economy with enough money to keep it operating smoothly, but by manipulating the amount of money available the Fed also controls interest rates—the price of "renting" money.

It's not too hard to understand that if something is out of whack in the economy and there seems to be movement toward a recession, then the Federal Reserve should be able to make more money available to banks to loan out to businesses (at lower interest rates) for investment in job-creating projects, or to consumers who would then be able to buy more cars, houses, and other things they may need or want. This should create more spending and more jobs and get the economy moving again.

By the same reasoning, if the economy is heating up and the rate of inflation is increasing beyond acceptable levels, then the Fed should be able to slow things down by making less money available to banks, who would then be forced to lend less to businesses and consumers. This tightening of the money supply would put the brakes on spending, which, in turn, slows the rate of inflation. The trade-off, of course, may be higher rates of unemployment.

To the extent that the Fed can pull off this balancing act, it should be able to engineer full employment without excessive inflation. This process, called **monetary policy,** is a major part of the arsenal of tools the monetary authorities have for controlling economic activity.

KEY CONCEPT: MONETARY POLICY IS THE FEDERAL RESERVE
BANK'S ABILITY TO CHANGE THE MONEY SUPPLY AND
INTEREST RATES TO INFLUENCE ECONOMIC ACTIVITY.

FISCAL POLICY

The government can also influence economic activity more directly through its abilities to spend and to tax. Again, in its simplest version, this process—called **fiscal policy**—is fairly easy to understand. The reason the federal government is so influential is that is accounts for roughly 23 percent of the total spending in the U.S. economy. That means that the government is a major force in keeping the economy running and providing jobs.

KEY CONCEPT: FISCAL POLICY IS THE GOVERNMENT'S ABILITY
TO INFLUENCE ECONOMIC BEHAVIOR BY CHANGING EITHER
THE LEVEL OF GOVERNMENT SPENDING OR THE RATE OF
TAXATION.

Taxes play an equally important role. The government's income, of course, comes from taxes. Taxes influence economic behavior directly, because when they are increased people have less money to spend on other things. On the other hand, when taxes are lowered, more money is made available for personal and business spending, which stimulates the economy and, in turn, affects the stock market.

This ability to increase or decrease government spending and to change tax rates allows the government to influence economic activity in a manner that is much more direct than the Fed's ability to influence economic activity through monetary policy.

If the economy seems to be sliding into a recession, the government can attempt to change its course by increasing government spending and lowering taxes. More government spending means more jobs are created. Lower taxes mean consumers have more money to spend. Both of these actions stimulate economic activity and should help get the economy moving again.

On the other hand, if the economy is moving too fast and inflation rates are excessive, the government can decrease spending and/or increase taxes. This will reduce the number of jobs available and reduce the amount of money consumers have to spend.

The overall effect of governmental fiscal policy is much the same as the effect of manipulating the money supply and interest rates. The economy can be slowed or stimulated if the right medicine is administered.

The central point of this very brief excursion into monetary and fiscal policy is that the economy can be controlled by appropriate action on the part of the central banking authorities and/or Congress, the president and federal agencies. However, what results is a very fragile balancing act between the trade-offs of unemployment and inflation. Policies designed to reduce unemployment tend to bring with them the undesirable effect of pushing up the rate of inflation. And using monetary and/or fiscal policy to slow down inflation almost always increases the rate of unemployment, and may also affect the stock market adversely. This is summarized in Table 6-2.

The challenge for economists and economic policy-makers is to determine how much of each is acceptable and then to steer the economy accordingly—while hoping that no one falls off the tightrope in the process. While this task is acknowledged by almost everyone, it is important to remember that there is much disagreement as to how it should be accomplished, or, indeed, whether it should even be attempted.

THE BATHTUB THEOREM

The same process can be explained in a simpler way, one that is perhaps easier to understand. Consider the economy from the perspective of what goes into it that creates jobs and incomes (injections) compared to what

Table 6-2:

MONETARY AND FISCAL POLICY

To stimulate the economy in times of recession, the government can:

FISCAL POLICY	MONETARY POLICY
1. Increase government spending	1. Increase the money supply
2. Decrease taxes	2. Lower the interest rate

To slow down the economy in times of inflation, the government can:

FISCAL POLICY	MONETARY POLICY
1. Decrease government spending	1. Decrease the money supply
2. Increase taxes.	2. Raise the interest rate

leaks out of it that eliminates jobs and lowers the overall level of income (leakages).

Imagine that an economy is represented by a bathtub with two faucets and two drains. Figure 6-1 shows it in cross section. One faucet represents inflows of investment into the economy— the tub in this case. The other faucet represents government spending. As the water (G and I) flows into the tub, jobs are generated. Suppose further that the level of water in the tub represents a level less than full employment, that is, less than 125 million jobs.

It's easy to see that if we add enough government spending and enough investment to the general level of economic activity already going on in the tub, then we can bring the water level

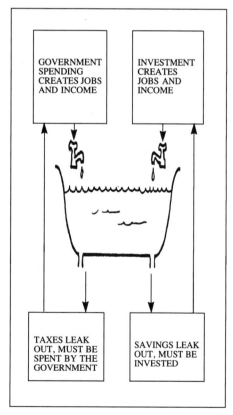

Figure 6-1, The Bathtub Theorem.

to full employment. As we have seen, this is one of the government's major goals. However, since the tub has two drains, one representing savings (S) and the other representing taxes (T), we can also see that not all of the added water will immediately increase the level of economic activity.

Whenever savings are taken out of the economy (the tub) jobs will be lost unless the savings are re-invested into the economy. By the same token, if taxes are taken out of income, less will be spent on consumption and jobs will be lost unless the government spends the tax revenues. If the savings and taxes are leaking out of the tub faster than the investment and government faucets are filling it, then the overall level of employment and economic activity will fall. That is, the water level will drop. On the other hand, if the G and I faucets are pumping water—money—into the tub faster than the T and S drains are letting it flow out, then the economy will have more jobs than it can handle, just as the tub has more water than it can handle. People will be demanding more goods than the economy can produce, and the result will be inflation.

Therefore, the government and the monetary authorities must constantly keep adjusting the faucets and the drains to achieve full employment without at the same time causing excessive inflation. This somewhat oversimplified way of looking at the economy and how it works is, appropriately enough, called the *injections* and *leakages* approach.

THE ECONOMY AND THE STOCK MARKET

What does this brief look at what makes the economy tick tell us about how the stock market may or may not perform? A lot. While, in the short-run, the market is often—in the short-run—more responsive to changes in interest rates than any other single factor, in the longer-run the stock market reflects the performance of the economy.

If it appears the economy is going to move into a recessionary phase, then stock traders expect company earnings to be falling and stock prices to fall with them. Of course, the reverse also is true. If the economy is expected to grow vigorously then company earnings and stock prices are likely to rise. This is why savvy investors follow the economy as well as the market as they develop their investment strategies. That, it turns out, is not as difficult as it might seem. All it involves is some elementary economic forecasting techniques.

ECONOMIC FORECASTING

Economic forecasting sounds like a complicated business, and it is, but there's an easy way to get a pretty good idea of what the economy is going to be up to: just watch the *Leading Economic Indicators*. The rationale behind the leading indicators is that studies have shown there are some economic indexes that usually show changes about six months before the economy does.

This useful planning tool came out of studies done by the National Bureau of Economic Research during the 1950s. The bureau studied some 800 statistical series and determined about 20 either turned up or down ahead of, with, or behind the business cycle. Out of those studies came what we now call the leading, coincident, and lagging indicators, which are the government's most important forecasting tools.

Of these, for someone just wanting to get an idea of what may be happening to the economy in the near future, the Leading Economic Indicators are the most interesting. Currently the Commerce Department tracks 11 statistical series, sums them into an index, and publishes the results at the end of each month.

The leading indicators include a wide range of things that reflect long-range business plans or expectations. At present they include: building permits, new consumer goods orders, the average hourly work week, new unemployment claims, inventory changes, the money supply, vendor delivery performance, some commodity prices, new plant and equipment contracts, and the performance of the stock market as measured by the Standard and Poor's 500 index, and others as shown in Table 6-3.

These series almost never move in the same direction at the same time but, when taken as a whole, they provide a pretty good gauge of where the economy is heading. The leading indicators have only been wrong three times in the past 30 years which, as economic forecasts go, is a pretty good track record.

Of all the indicators the overall performance of the stock market—not just the Dow Jones average—is probably the best leading indicator, but just watching it alone is not enough. The market, Nobel-laureate economist Paul Samuelson once quipped, "has predicted nine of the last five recessions." Nonetheless, the market does seem to have an uncanny knack for signaling economic turndowns. This is because it reflects how investors perceive the economic effects of political developments, what investors think about corporate profit prospects, and how interest rates may affect the economy.

Table 6-3

STATISTICS THAT FORECAST THE ECONOMY

Economists watch the Index of Leading Economic Indicators to see what the economy will be doing during the next six months. The index takes into account the 11 statistics shown here:

Index of Leading Economic Indicators—The main index that includes the 11 others shown below

Manufacturing Labor Hours—Average hours employees work per week.

Unemployment Claims—Weekly claims on unemployment insurance

New Consumer Goods Orders—Orders for manufacturing, consumer goods and materials

Delayed Deliveries—Percent firms getting delayed deliveries

Consumer Confidence—Consumer expectations of economy's health

Building Permits—Monthly total building permits issued

Commodity Prices—Change in sensitive materials prices.

Stock Prices—500 common stocks

Money Supply M2—Real money supply, month average

New Plants & Equipment—Contracts and orders, plant and equipment

Unfilled Orders for Durables—Change in manufacturers unfilled orders for durable goods

SOURCE: Department of Commerce.

We've had eleven recessions between World War II and the early 1990s. The market—as measured by the Standard and Poor's index—has started to decline on the average nine months before each. It has only failed to signal bad times ahead twice in the past 60 years. Once was in early 1980; the other was in 1929.

So, if you are going to be a serious investor, one of the things you need to do is keep an eye on the economy. One way to do this is watch interest rates and, especially, what the Fed is up to. If the Fed is pushing interest rates down that's probably good news; if it is pursuing "tight money" policies, pushing interest rates up, that's almost certainly bad news if you are invested in the stock market.

The other thing to watch is what the federal government is up to. If government spending is being increased, that will most likely stimulate the economy and be good news for the stock market; if the government is cutting spending, that may be bad news for the market.

However, because of concerns over the size of the federal deficits in recent years, the market has sometimes reacted favorably to news that government spending was being cut. Why? Because less government spending means less government borrowing, and that means interest rates will probably fall as there is less demand for money from the government. Which brings us back to the point that when it comes to the economy *and* the stock market *interest rates are the key to almost everything*.

Finally, watching indexes like the Leading Economic Indicators, which are widely-publicized, is an easy way to keep an eye on the economy's prospects. If the leading indicators fall for three or more months in a row, that's a reliable signal that the economy may be turning downward.

LOOKING AHEAD

Now that we've completed our journey through the details of investing in the financial markets—with some emphasis on the stock market—it seems appropriate to step back and review what we have seen along the way. Then we leave you with a few tips that may be of value.

Chapter 7:

The Main Points

Now that we have examined the details of investing in the financial markets it seems appropriate to pause and recap what we have learned. This chapter summarizes the important points and provides some axioms worth considering if you want to be a happy investor. Then we close with some "hot tips" on how to avoid making a major and costly mistake in your investment strategy.

In Chapter 1 we took a brief trip into the real world of investing in the stock market by buying some fictitious stocks and following our portfolio through a typical year. The reason we opened the book that way was that we wanted to emphasize that there is nothing mysterious about investing in the stock market.   ☞ ALL YOU HAVE TO DO IS FIND A RELIABLE STOCK-BROKER.

Then we tried to emphasize that it is a myth that you have to have a lot of money to invest in stocks. This is a psychological barrier for many people that prevents some from beginning an investment program when they should. Most stockbrokers are willing—if not eager—to talk to anyone, even people who only have a small amount to invest.   ☞ DON'T BE INTIMI-DATED BY THE MYTH THAT YOU HAVE TO HAVE A LOT OF MONEY TO INVEST IN THE STOCK MARKET.

Then we tried to emphasize that diversifying your portfolio is an important way to reduce risk. That means mixing your investments among several different stocks and perhaps considering a mutual fund, which is diversified by definition.   ☞ DIVERSITY TO REDUCE RISK.

Finally, we made the point that if nothing else, savvy investors must learn how to follow their investments. That means learning how to read the

117

stock tables and devising a way to keep records of how your investments are doing. ☞ LEARN HOW TO READ THE STOCK TABLES AND KEEP RECORDS.

Then in Chapter 2 we took a brief excursion into how the system that allows investors to participate in the profits of corporations works. That system, capitalism, encourages entrepreneurs to take risks to start new companies with the hope of making profits for themselves and others. They do this by putting up their own money or by inviting others to share in the risk and to participate by issuing and selling new stocks. ☞ WHEN YOU BUY STOCK IN A NEW COMPANY YOU OWN PART OF IT AND HAVE A SAY IN HOW IT IS MANAGED—BUT YOU ALSO GET TO SHARE IN THE RISKS.

If you are going to be an entrepreneur you have to deal with a number of logistical questions, assuming that you want to run a public company with outside investors. Among these are establishing a board of directors to oversee your operations and represent the stockholders. Also, being a public company involves having your operations watched over by the securities and Exchange Commission, which means you have to file financial reports.

From an investor's point of view the most important financial reports a company issues are the income statement and the balance sheet. ☞ LEARN HOW TO READ AND INTERPRET FINANCIAL STATEMENTS.

Finally, we emphasized that everyone has an interest in stock prices, especially the managers who share in the profits and who gain from increases in stock prices—or lose a lot, perhaps even lose their jobs, if stock prices fall.

In Chapter 3 we highlighted our conviction that if you want to understand anything it's important to understand its history. This took us into a brief excursion into the history of how the stock market and the various stock exchanges evolved. We then looked at the various exchanges and their functions, and at other kinds of investment opportunities such as bonds and commodities. And we examined the different sources of information about such investments found in the financial pages of most newspapers. This included the bond market, U.S. Treasury securities, commodities exchanges and stock index futures. The point to remember here is that bonds represent a relatively secure way to invest because they have a fixed rate of return, but they are also risky in the sense that bond prices change as interest rates change. ☞ BONDS ARE A RELATIVELY SAFE INVESTMENT, BUT THEY ARE SUBJECT TO CAPITAL GAINS OR LOSSES AS INTEREST RATES FLUCTUATE. THEREFORE THEY ARE NOT RISK FREE.

Investing in commodities and other more complicated and risky areas like futures contracts is the province of the professional investor. To be sure, one can make a lot of money fast, but you can lose it even faster.
☞ LEAVE COMMODITIES AND FUTURES MARKETS TO THE PROS.

Chapter 4 looked at mutual funds—the easy way to invest in the market—and bank savings accounts. Given that there are more mutual funds—more than 4,000—than there are individual stocks listed on the New York Stock Exchange, there are a lot of options. The problem here is to find a fund that has goals consistent with your own investment strategy and needs. Once you do put your money in, be patient, most mutual funds have a good record over time. ☞ MUTUAL FUNDS ARE THE EASIEST WAY TO INVEST IN THE MARKET.

The proper mix of mutual funds and other kinds of investments is another question. Most financial advisors suggest taking a relatively aggressive growth strategy if you are young and want to build a retirement portfolio. Then as you get older you should shift your investments into more secure areas even if it involves lower rates of return. But, in any case, keep some of your portfolio invested in growth stocks in order to keep ahead of inflation. ☞ THE PROPER PORTFOLIO MIX DEPENDS ON YOUR AGE AND YOUR GOALS.

Putting your money in the bank in a savings account or a certificate of deposit is, of course, the safest way to invest your money and everyone should have some of their investments stashed safely in the bank. The issue here is that unless your investment increases in value faster than the rate of inflation you're pretty much standing still, while paying taxes on the interest you receive to boot. ☞ PUTTING YOUR MONEY IN THE BANK IS THE SAFEST WAY TO INVEST.

Finally, its important to remember that all investments tend to grow faster than their stated rate of return if you reinvest your dividends or interest. That's because of compounding—earning interest on interest. Over the long run the results of compounding are dramatic. ☞ DON'T OVERLOOK THE POWER OF COMPOUNDING.

Chapter 5 took us into a different ball game, investing the hard way by being your own stock picker. This involves two very important factors: one, you need to know what you are doing, and two, you need to have the time to spend on it. Time, it is important to recognize, is money for most of us. But, given that, if you want to manage your own portfolio there are some basic ways to do it.

☞ IF YOU WANT TO MANAGE YOUR OWN PORTFOLIO BE SURE YOU
HAVE THE KNOWLEDGE AND TIME TO DO IT.

Fundamental analysis is the most basic of all investment strategies. It
involves studying companies' financial records, and especially their earnings
and dividend history, and trying to make intelligent choices about their
future. This means you have to know how to read income statements and
balance sheets, among other things. ☞ START WITH FUNDAMENTAL
ANALYSIS.

If you want to get more sophisticated you can try technical analysis,
which means trying to chart and analyze stock trends using a myriad of
techniques. In essence, charting involves trying to out guess the psychology
of the market—not an easy task. Technical analysis is a game for those who
like to play with charts and computers and for those who believe that history
repeats itself. But there is not a lot of evidence that it does a much better
job of predicting stock ups and downs than fundamental analysis and common sense. In some cases, however, it may be useful—if you have a lot of
time on your hands. ☞ TECHNICAL ANALYSIS MAY BE USEFUL, BUT
PROBABLY TAKES MORE TIME THAN IT'S WORTH.

But before you get too bogged down in fundamental and technical analysis you might want to consider that the random walk theory says that
nobody can really do a very good job of picking stocks. Indeed, in a number
of tests, throwing darts at the stock tables has proved to be about as good
a way to pick stocks as any. This is because there is so much knowledge
out there about every company that is listed on the exchanges and so many
people watching them that the market efficiently adjusts to any new information. That has led some to think that the best bet is to simply invest in
the stock market index funds, which only try to match the performance of
the overall market. ☞ BECAUSE THE MARKET IS A RANDOM WALK YOU
MAY DO JUST AS WELL BY PLAYING THE STOCK INDEX FUNDS.

Beyond all that, there are a number of ways to get sophisticated when
you are serving as your own investment advisor. You can buy warrants and
options, you can sell "short," or you can borrow money and buy on "margin." These are games for the rich, the stout-hearted, and the profession-
als.They allow you to make money fast—and to lose it even faster.
☞ LEAVE WARRANTS, OPTIONS, SHORT SELLING, AND BUYING ON MARGIN
TO THE PROFESSIONALS.

In Chapter 6 we reminded you again that if you are going to be a
serious investor you need to be able to keep track of what's going on. This

means you have to understand the various stock indexes, and you have to know how the economy affects the performance of the market.

So, you need to watch the Dow-Jones Industrial Average, which is designed to give a quick snapshot of how the market is doing, based on the performance of thirty selected stocks—all large companies. But you need to remember that the Dow may not tell you much about your own particular portfolio, especially if you invest only in smaller company stocks, and that it is not adjusted for inflation. ☞ THE DOW IS A USEFUL INDICATOR OF MARKET PERFORMANCE, BUT IT DOESN'T TELL AS MUCH AS OTHER MEASURES OF THE MARKET.

Much more useful indexes of market performance are the broader indexes, such as the Standard & Poor's 500 and the Wilshire Index. Because it takes a broad spectrum of stocks in several different exchanges, the S & P 500 is probably the one to watch if you are interested in overall market performance. ☞ KEEP AN EYE ON THE STANDARD & POOR'S 500.

When it comes to following the economy and trying to figure out its relationship to the stock market, the problem is more complicated. In the short run the market can do well even if the economy is slipping. But in the long run if the economy doesn't do well it's going to affect the stock market—and a lot of other things. The key here is keeping an eye on interest rates and what the Federal Reserve Bank and the government itself are up to. Interest rates are the most important because they affect other investment options. ☞ IF INTEREST RATES ARE FALLING THAT'S GOOD NEWS FOR THE STOCK MARKET. IF THEY ARE RISING IT'S BAD NEWS FOR THE MARKET AND THE ECONOMY.

Also, astute investors need to have some way to forecast what is going to happen to the economy in the future. No one can predict that with any degree of certainty—especially not professional economists. But, one relatively simple way to do it and save yourself a lot of time is to watch the government's Index of Leading Economic Indicators, which is designed to predict what the economy is going to be doing six months down the road. The indicators are not infallible, but are right more often than not. Beyond that, you can consult the tea leaves.

Finally, here are a few tips you might want to consider. They are not "hot" stock market tips; just common sense. And they are not very likely to make you rich, but ignoring them could be costly. For starters, the basics:

● Don't invest in the stock market at all unless you have enough money set aside to cover all your normal living expenses for at least 6 months, a solid retirement plan, and life and medical insurance programs.

● Don't pay any attention to hot tips, inside information, rumors, and the like. Anything that sounds too good to be true probably is.

● Figure out where you want to land before you jump. If you don't know what you're looking for, you'll have a hard time finding it.

● Don't put all your eggs in one basket. Diversify your investment portfolio. Put part in common stocks, part in bonds, and part in bank CDs. The right mix depends on your aversion to risk.

● The easiest way to diversity is to invest in a mutual fund. It's a simple way to get your toe in the water while, at the same time, letting the professionals worry about the rest.

● If you're young and trying to accumulate a retirement nest egg, be aggressive and lean toward common stocks. If you're retired, stick to more conservative investments, such as Treasury bonds and long term bank certificates of deposit.

● But, remember that if you aren't beating the rate of inflation, you're actually losing money.

● Also, remember that sometimes the market goes down. When it does, that's a good time to buy.

● Investing a set amount of money in stocks every month eliminates the problem of having to worry about when to buy, and you come out ahead of the averages over the long run.

Then, the subtleties:

● Put a small part of your investments in something risky, but not more than you can afford to lose without having to lower your standard of living.

● Don't deal with "cold calls" from people trying to sell you stock. They usually come from inexperienced brokers or experienced con men.

● Don't forget that stockbrokers are in business to make money, which they do by buying and selling stocks for you and charging you a commission. Nonetheless, a good stock broker can be invaluable.

● If you are investing directly in the stock market, don't ever turn control of your investments over to anyone else.

● Develop a stock picking style, then stick to it.

● Focus on the future, not the past. The past is history and history doesn't always repeat itself. Losers come back.

● Don't buy on margin. You can make money faster by borrowing to buy stocks; you can also lose it faster, along with everything else you've got.

• Leave commodities, futures, options, puts, calls, and the like, to the professionals. Double that for the foreign exchange markets.

• Remember—*nobody* can predict the market. Anybody who says he can is a charlatan.

• If you find something good, hang on to it, and buy more.

• Buy stocks when they are cheap. Figure out what price/earnings ratios mean. And remember that stock with a low price/earnings ratio is not necessarily the best buy.

• Keep track of your investments, be prepared to sell, and use stop-loss orders.

Finally, remember that people seeking financial advice are best advised to consult a registered financial planner who doesn't have anything to sell except advice. And, when it comes to tips, consider your source. That applies, especially, to all of the above.

Suggested Further Reading:

The Wall Street Journal guide to Understanding Money & Markets, Accesspress, Simon & Schuster. (1990)

A Random Walk Down Wall Street, Burton G. Malkiel, W.W. Norton & Company. (1990)

Black Monday, Tim Metz. William Morrow & Company, Inc. (1988)

The New York Times Guide to Mutual Funds, Carole Gould. Times Books, Random House. (1992)

The Instant Economist, John Charles Pool and Ross M. LaRoe. Addison-Wesley. (1985)

Keys to Risks and Rewards of Penny Stocks, Robert L. Frick and Mary Lynne Vellinga. Barrons Education Series. (1990)

How to Read and Profit From Financial News, Gerald Krefetz. Ticknor & Fields. (1984)

Understanding Common Stocks, Phyllis C. Kaufman and Arnold Corrigan. Longmeadow Press. (1987)

How to Read the Financial Pages, Peter Passell. Warner Books. (1986)

Family Investment Guide, John Dorfman. Jove. (1984)

How to Buy Stocks, Louis Engel and Brendan Boyd. Bantam. (1987)

Understanding Wall Street, Jeffery B. Little and Lucien Rhodes. McGraw-Hill. (1991)

How to be Your Own Stockbroker, Charles Schwab. Dell. (1984)

Dun & Bradstreet: Guide to $Your Investments$, Nancy Dunnan. Harper Collins. (1993)

Guide to Understanding Personal Finance, Kenneth M. Morris and Alan M. Seigel. Lightbulb Press. (1992)

Portfolio Worksheet

COMPANY _____

DATE	PRICE	NO. SHARES	LONG VALUE	PERCENT CHANGE	PERCENT GAIN	GAIN OR LOSS

Portfolio Worksheet

COMPANY _____

DATE	PRICE	NO. SHARES	LONG VALUE	PERCENT CHANGE	PERCENT GAIN	GAIN OR LOSS